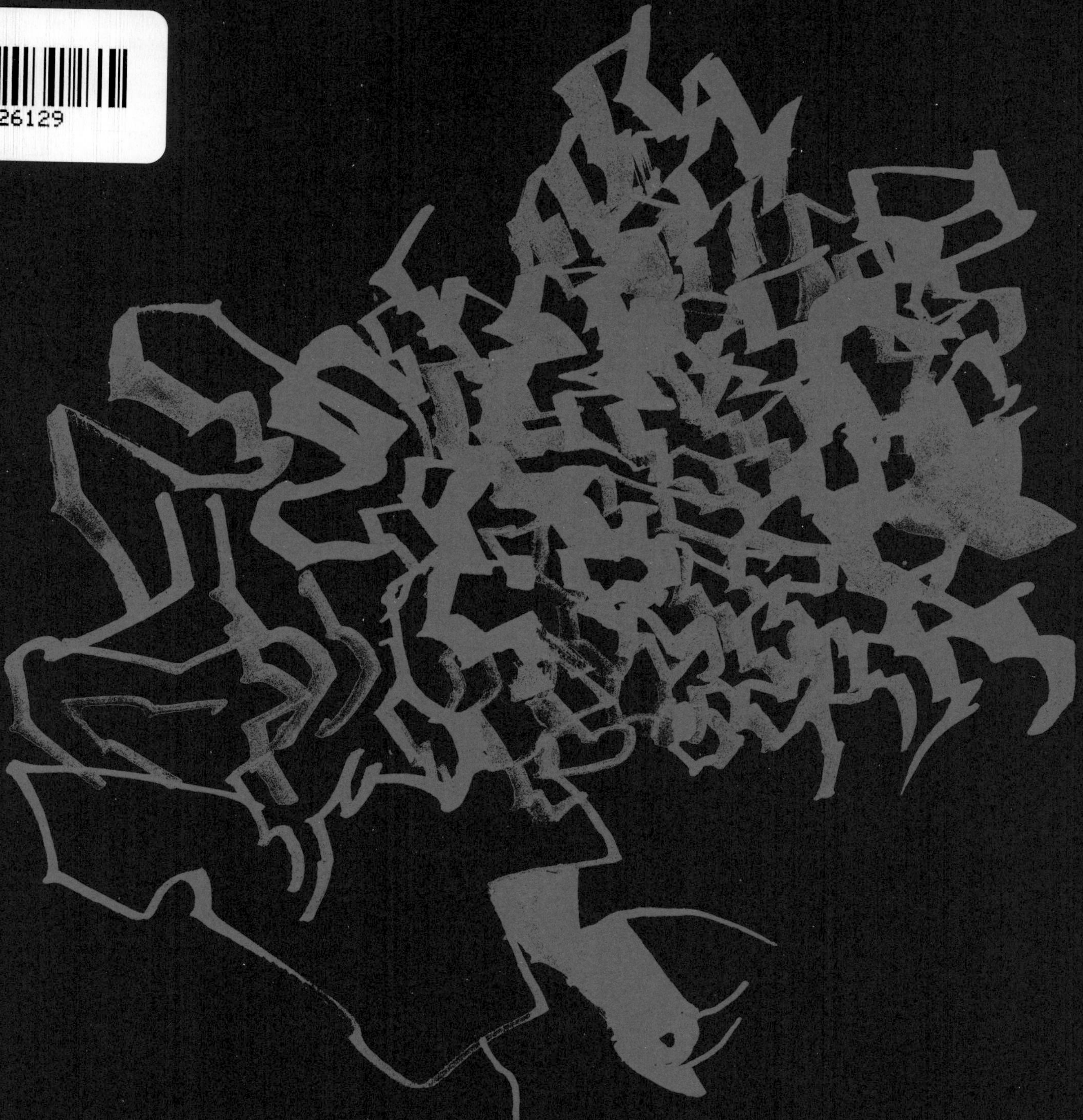

MUÑOZ & SAMPAYO

BILLIE HOLIDAY

nbm GRAPHIC NOVELS
Nantier • Beall • Minoustchine
NEW YORK

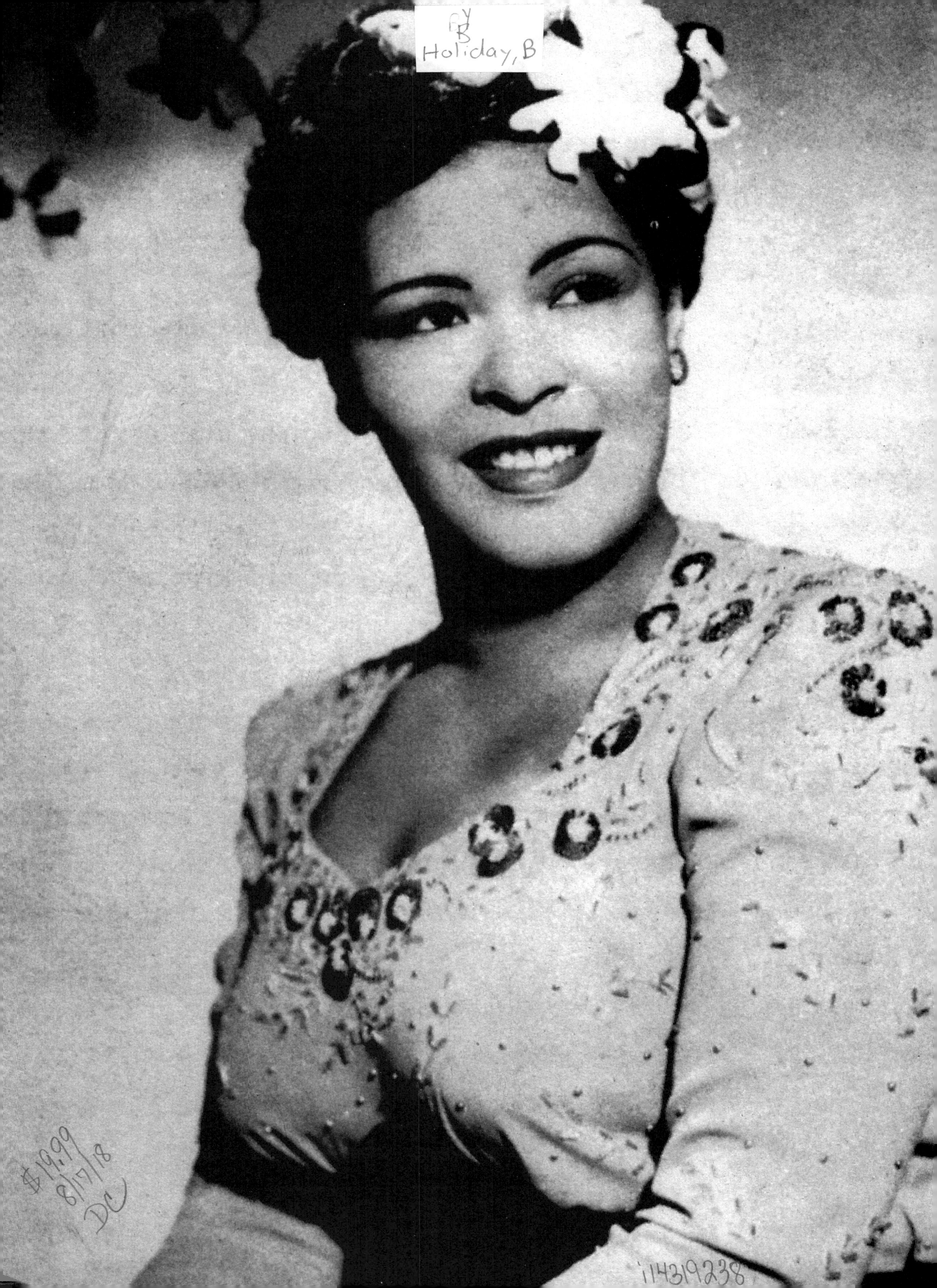

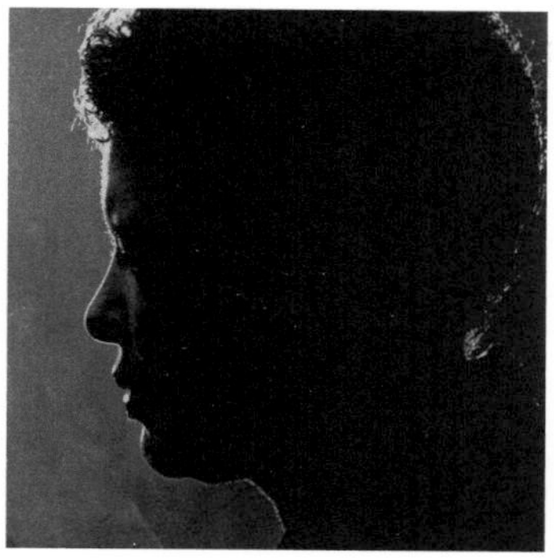

BILLIE HOLIDAY: DON'T EXPLAIN

Let's forget for a moment, please, since it's unforgettable in of itself, in fact, impossible, indelible, but *try* to forget her mother giving birth at the age of thirteen, her great-grandmother housed in a shack in the back of the plantation, whom the master, a handsome Irishman, would come bang at set times, and by whom she would have seventeen children all dead except for one, Billie's grandfather. Let's forget her grandmother who died while holding the child so tightly they had to break her arm. Let's forget her being raped at the age of fourteen, the little slut. Let's forget her being rejected by everybody, the misery, the foulness of men, the slammer, those well-made asylums meant for rehabbing you, the cops, and that mess of white powder washed down with scotch. Billie Holiday got lucky. She had more money than all the black women in America put together. She wore diamonds, furs. What people remember about her is her laughter, that of a child and a spoiled woman, a knowing burst of laughter. The laughter of life.

She even knew cheerfulness and happiness, but only barely, as if in passing. It's just that she experienced them with such an intensity, so electrically, including through the powders, that she dived into it much further than anyone else. There was no downward slope in Billie Holiday that would lead her to anything worse. Those are fables concocted by men bereft of imagination. After all, her existence continually got off to bad starts. In her lifetime, people exploited her to the bone, creating off her hide the myth upon which jazz nourishes as well as smothers itself.

Her jazz image in black and white: her airs of an earthy lowlife lout whom people hated at first was the epitome of racism. This was then greatly mythologized with the breathless expatiation of fans whom people are now trying to whitewash with a barrage of sociology and anthropology and with a big gloss of puritanical morality.

Photos on top and opposite page: ©Archives Francis Paudras

Billie Holiday, lucky for her, had multiple lives, several simultaneous, crisscrossed lives mixed up like threads in a skein, with enough amazing pleasures to convey them to everyone, with that laughter despite everything, against a backdrop of death, and that frenzied taste for men that eventualy dooms you, with the energy to live all those lives, each one a thousand times more than our hobbled, punctilious, bumpy lives. Lived above all with the ruinous capacity to live them all at once, to live them in the knots, in their breaches, their unbearable wounds. She died at the age of forty-four.

People did everything to her. She'd been raped as often as you can be raped without getting killed. She'd been locked up in all those buildings constructed to imprison madmen and delinquents—Negroes, too, who, often, if you handle it right, are a combo of the two. They supplied her with the powder of happiness and death that they then searched her pockets for, in order to convict her of possession. She was barred from New York clubs because of those convictions. Imagine that. A society in which she was, without a doubt, the sweetest, happiest, best-meaning apparition, spitefully banned Billie Holiday from the stage.

They prohibited her everything. It leaves you speechless but nothing ever did manage to keep her from singing. Nothing forever could cut off her beauty or her laughter, or keep her voiceless.

Eleonora Holiday, known as Billie or Lady Day, an American singer born in Philadelphia on April 7, 1915, who died in a New York hospital on July 17, 1959, is one of the voices of the century. There aren't many female voices that have her cry, her suffering, her rhythm, the hint of pleasure or that infinite beauty of pent-up love: Maria Callas, Oum Kalthoum, Edith Piaf, Billie Holiday.

People always dwell on the dark tragedy of Billie Holiday's life. It does jump out at you. But it may also give you distance. That's how you protect yourself in some sort of way.

Silently, you wonder: how did she keep going? And, then you can avoid the real, agonizing question: what kind of laughter was hers amid this repeated agony?

What kind of enjoyment could it have been against this backdrop? From what wellspring came that energy to create jazz in those seedy dives that sucked her in?

For Lady Day wasn't just a voice, a body, a lady hired to sing the blues (*Lady Sings the Blues* is the title of her autobiography). She is, more subtly, the main actress of that musical history with hints of frivolity and carelessness that people blandly label as jazz. Quite simply, she is an exceptional musician, on a par with Mozart or Stravinsky. Just as she's a writer using meaningless, little, everyday words that she twists in her mouth, on a par with Virginia Woolf, Carson McCullers, Marguerite Duras. This stature was established quickly.

No society was ever wrong about her many lives, oh, no. Not that of public order and decency that squeezed her. Nor that of

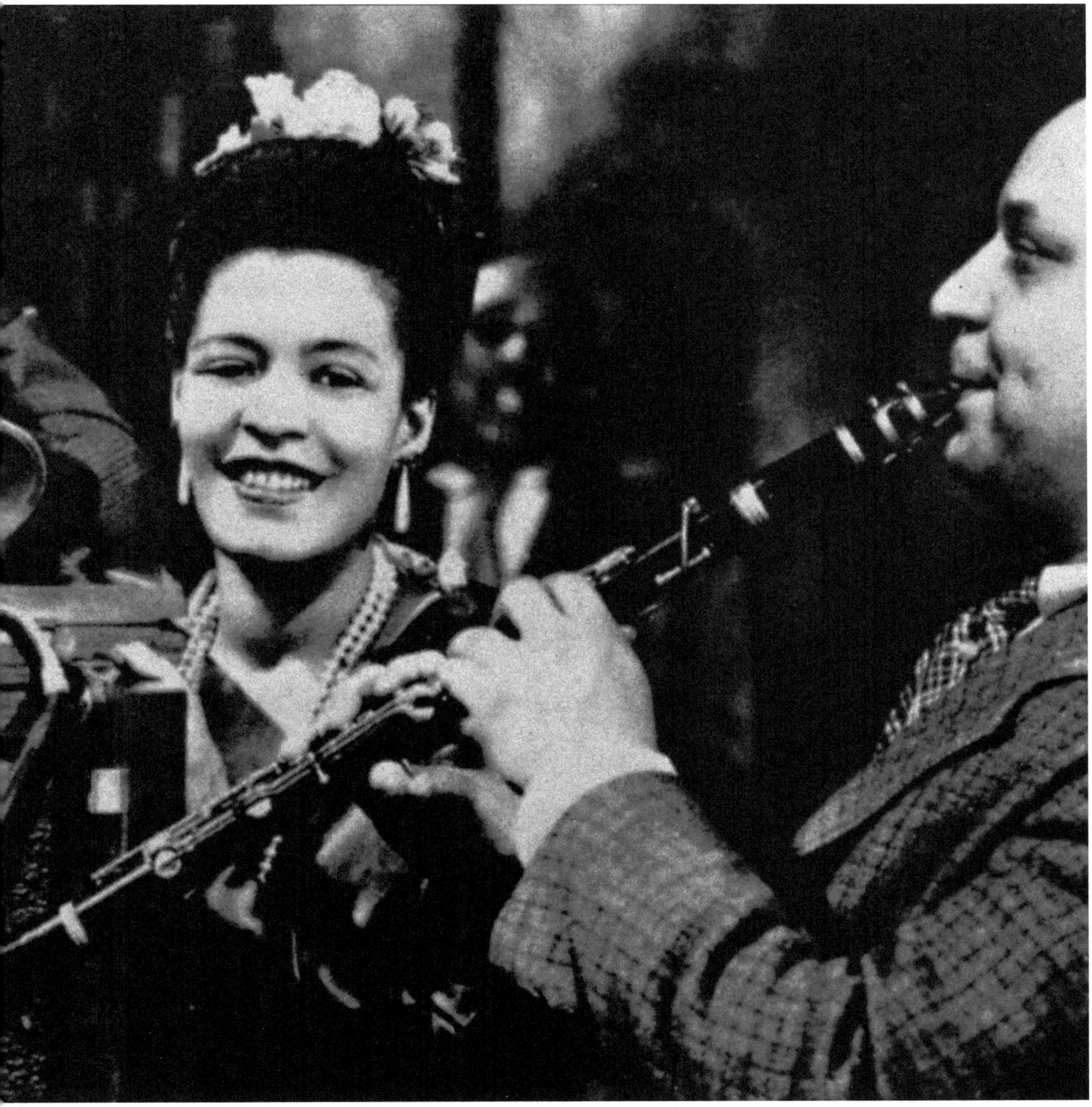

Louis Armstrong, Billie Holiday, and Barney Bigard in Arthur Lubin's New Orleans, 1947. *© Archives Francis Paudras.*

musicians, which welcomed her like a queen. She made her debut with Benny Goodman, before tackling the circuit of big clubs, finally crowned by Harlem's Apollo Theater. In 1935, she did a movie with Ellington. With Teddy Wilson, the prince of the piano, she met the most ethereal of soloists, all the uninhibited poets in a generation that unassumingly invented the music of tomorrow: Ben Webster, Roy Elridge, Harry Carney, Johnny

Hodges, and the greatest of them all: Lester Young, whom she would nickname "Prez" (President), while he coins "Lady Day" for her. They both fly away, unbeknownst to the world, into a (no doubt incomprehensible) secret of love and strangeness understood by no one, a parallel delirium reserved to themselves alone, extraordinary, beyond the stupidity and vulgarity of simple mortals.

Billie Holiday, Lester Young (saxophone), Coleman Hawkins (saxophone) and Gerry Mulligan (saxophone), during the program The Sound of Jazz, *CBS TV broadcast, December 1957. ©Collection F. Driggs/Magnum Photos Collection.*

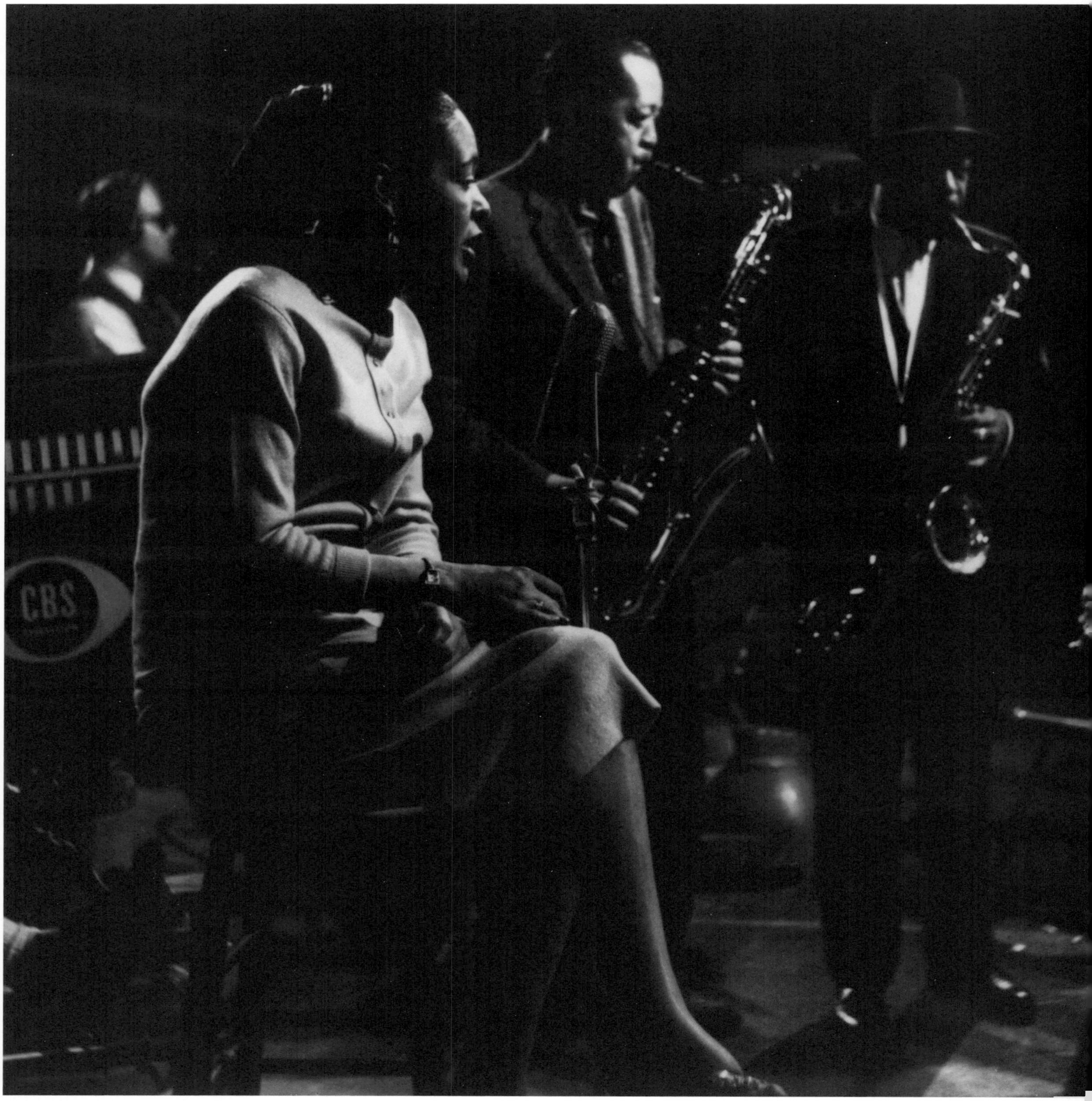
CBS

Lady Day knew, with a systematic knack in her choice aiding in her downfall, the most despicable and odious of men.

She tried to love them. They battered and bruised her. But she knew Lester like nobody else knew him. Maybe that was worth a few brutes.

That was his story, in any case. Whenever he spoke, Lester Young didn't talk like the rest of us. He murmured phrases with a strange ring to them. They were truer, more refined than ours are. Whenever he played, it truly was like an angel's flight. Prez's counterpoints to Lady Day's words are the most delicate, most audacious thing invented in the realm of exchanges between a man and a woman.

It was a pure duet of love that the confused thereafter dare to interpret as some sort of women's revenge. They wouldn't have understood anything about Angela Davis. Not even wondering what it was that each of the greatest musicians, and among them, the greatest of the great, the "musicians' musician," were seeking at the Café Society nightclub where Lady Day continued to sing: nothing! The glory of accompanying her, the chance to be her sideman for a moment, and the hope of reaching, who knows, the cutting edge of that writing-made-voice that's hers, which she alone could sing.

Billie Holiday was the singer that the big bands wanted. Their infatuation is understandable. A big band of the era—such as those of Jimmie Lunceford, Fletcher Henderson, Artie Shaw, Benny Carter, Count Basie (1937)—is unforgiving. They don't make mistakes. From a poem by Lewis Allan (Abel Meeropol, a teacher of Jewish roots and a member of the American Communist Party), Billie Holiday composed her 1939 ballad about hanged men, the awful fruit of lynching, "*Strange Fruit.*"

She becomes a star, very demanding about the "lyrics," records "*Lover Man,*" writes "*God Bless the Child*" (1941), and causes a scandal with "*Gloomy Sunday.*" Her studio partners include Roy Eldridge, Barney Bigard, Coleman Hawkins, Jack Teagarden, Art Tatum, Oscar Pettiford, the jazz elite of the Forties. The film industry, which never makes mistakes about African Americans, casts her as a singing maid alongside Louis Armstrong in *New Orleans* (1947). How funny. From there, she alternates with accelerated speed between the stages of the great theaters (Carnegie Hall) and those prisons, sanatoriums, and institutions that don't do her any good.

TV which, from its start, doesn't make any mistakes either, tapes in 1953—after her sessions with Stan Getz—an episode of *Comeback Story* which heavy-handedly puts in place that unfortunate image of the abyss and death.

It must be said that it was infinitely harder, no doubt, to approach her melodic genius, that twisting of sounds that prosecutes the lines of a text, its inner truth, its experience, because, like Bacon, she seems to be disfiguring a face. It's hard to approach that brilliant expressivity—gained, through limited means—that keeps her at the edge of being.

With "*Stormy Blues,*" "*Don't Explain,*" "*Lover Man,*" "*Left Alone*" and, step by step, in all the twists and turns of her voice, its halting languidness like broken joints, Billie Holiday carries the poetry of love to its extreme point of heartbreak and swallowed violence. She reveals in *The Sound of Jazz* (CBS, 1957), as she does in her autobiography (*Lady Sings the Blues*), the secret, bared thread of her passage on earth. She never performed the blues strictly speaking. The word, however, pops up in her titles and lyrics, but like a clue, an appeal, as a sharp point of suffering.

In 1958, she's in Paris. You might think she's adrift. Françoise Sagan, who loved her laugh ever since that crazy transatlantic trip that brought her to hear Holiday at Eddie Condon's in Connecticut, comes to see her. When she sings then, she mixes up verses, invents her memory, remakes the order of the world in her music. It makes you suffer from it. It shakes you completely to the core. Billie Holiday says this to Sagan, who takes it as an offhand bitter or cruel remark: "Anyhow, Darling, you know I am going to die very soon in New York, between two cops."

And that, believe it or not, is exactly what happens. In April 1959, she sings at Boston's Storyville nightclub—since New York has closed its clubs to her!—with Mal Waldron, Champ Jones, and Roy Haynes.

In May, she has her last appearance at the Phoenix Theater. On the 31st, she's in the hospital. She's indicted one last time. On her deathbed. She dies between two cops.

Francis Marmande

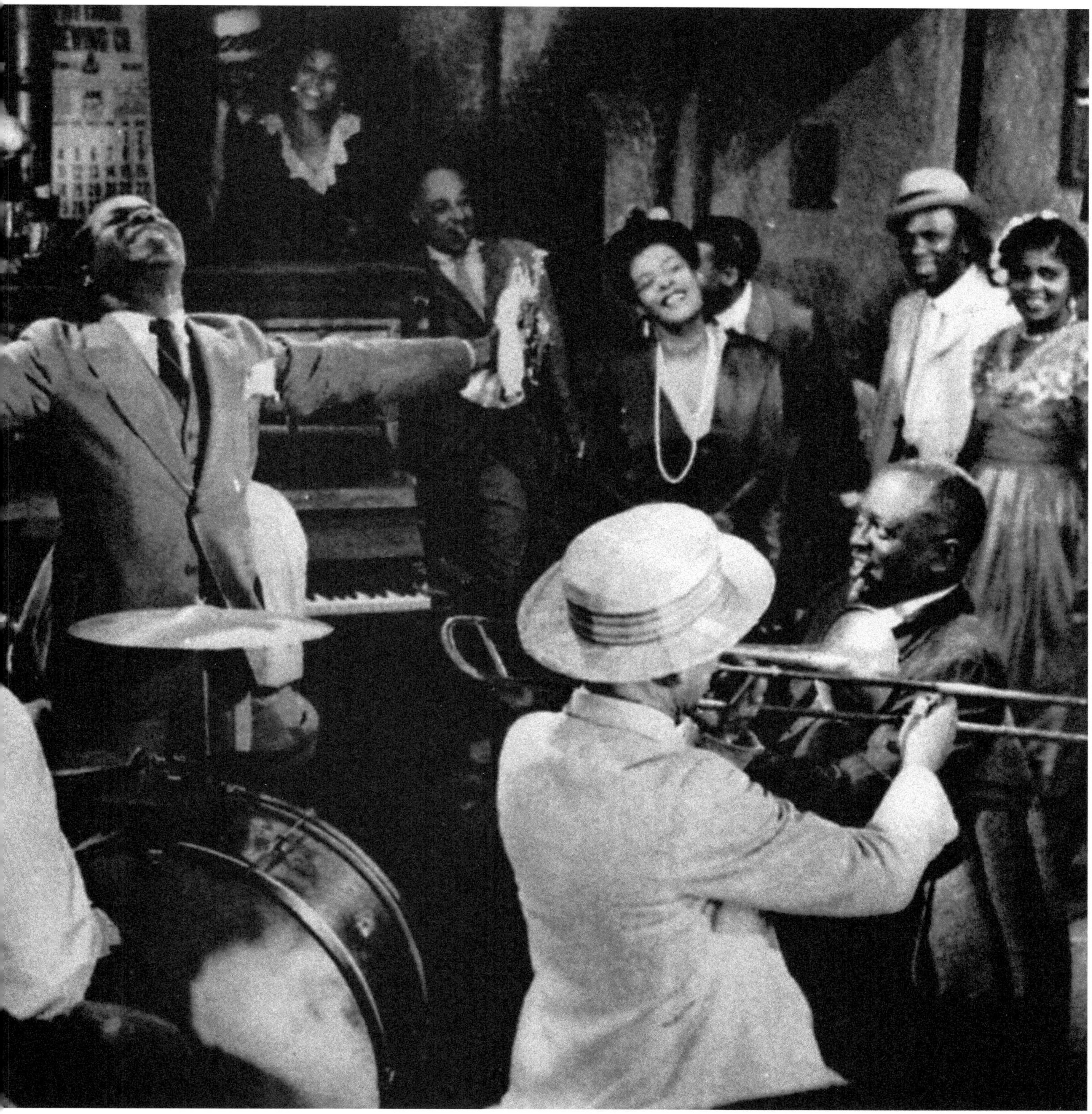

Red Calender (bass), Louis Armstrong (trumpet), Billie Holiday and Kid Ory (trombone) in New Orleans. *© Archives Francis Paudras*

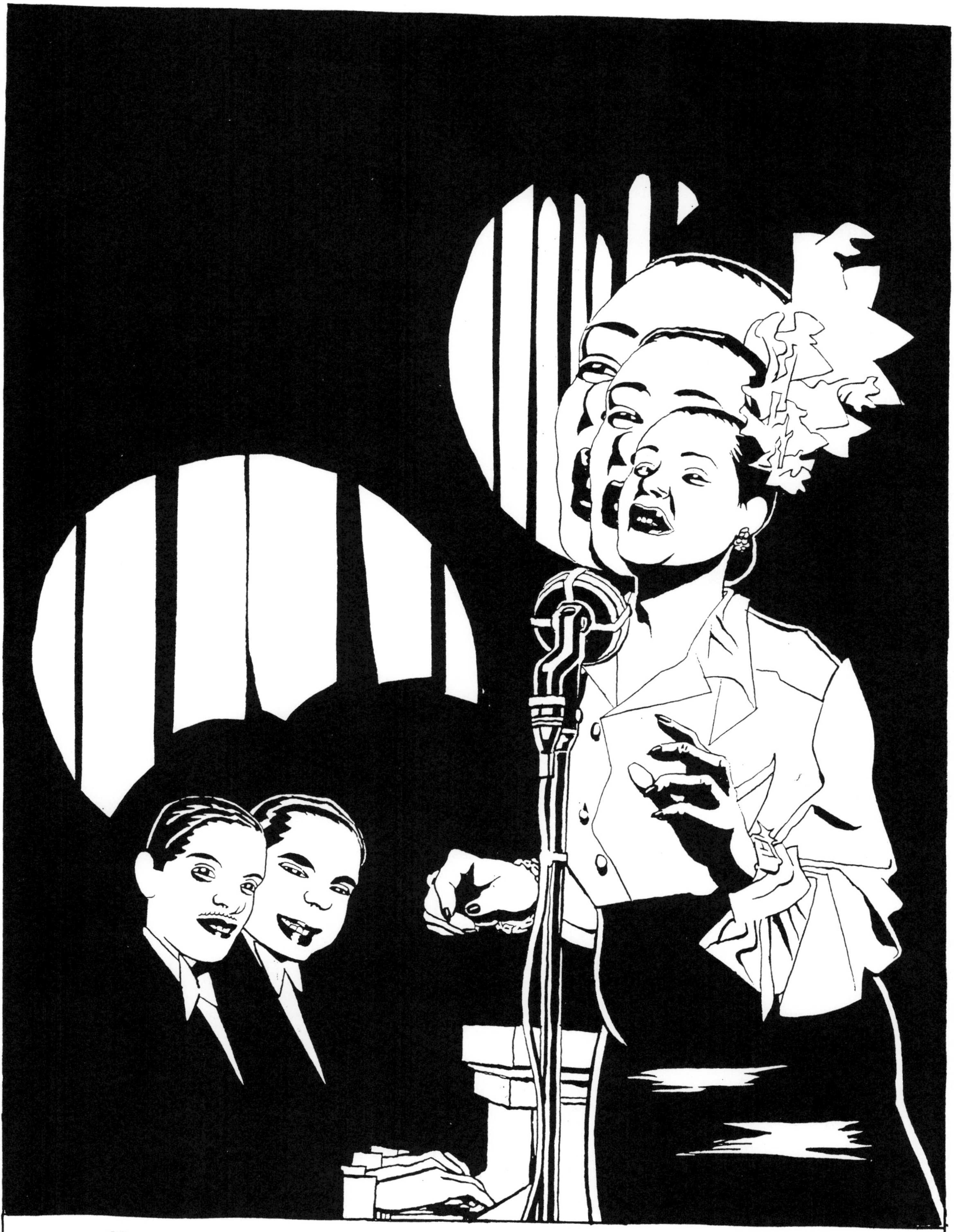
MUÑOZ
SAMPAYO

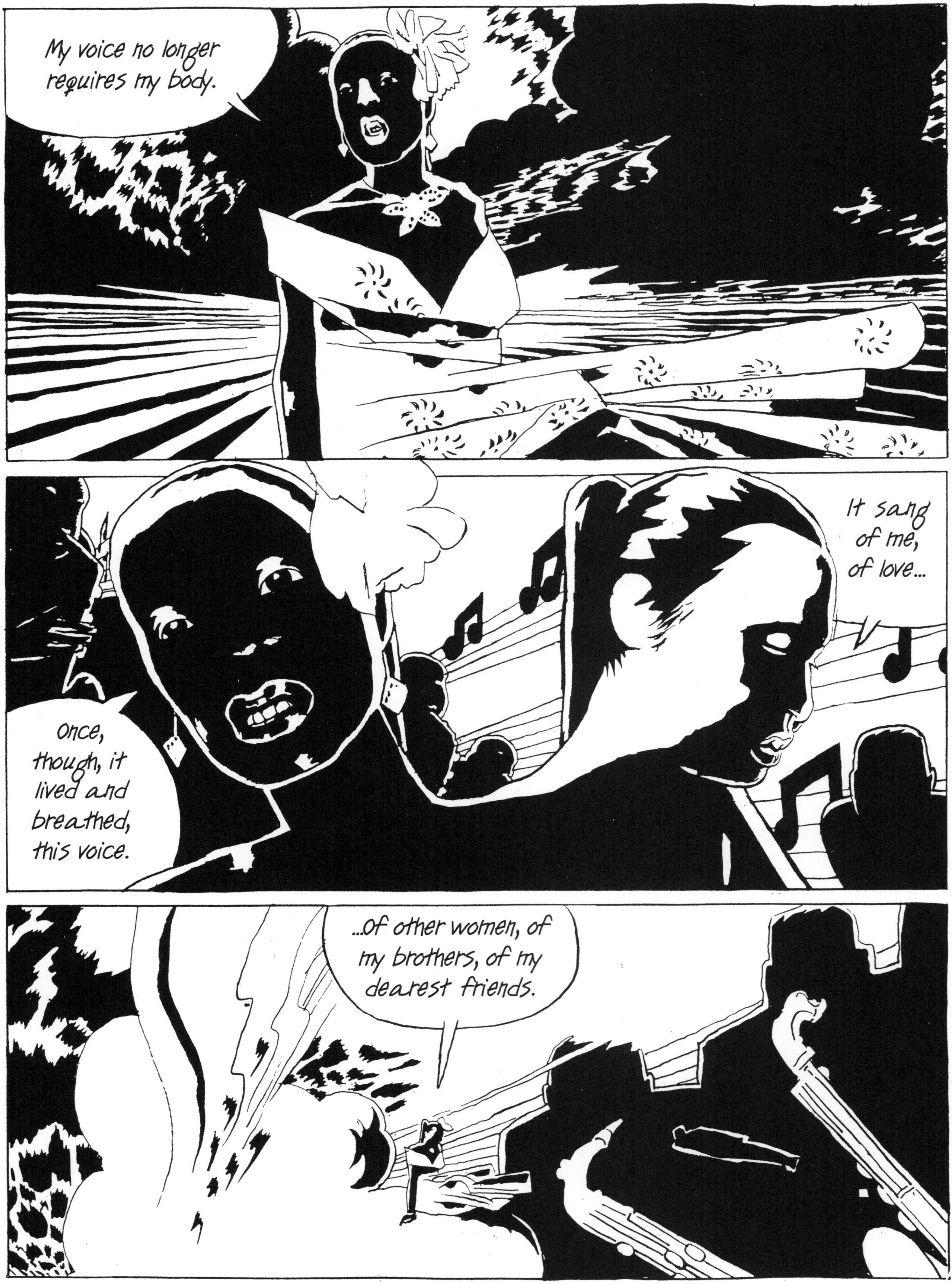
My voice no longer requires my body.
Once, though, it lived and breathed, this voice.
It sang of me, of love...
...of other women, of my brothers, of my dearest friends.

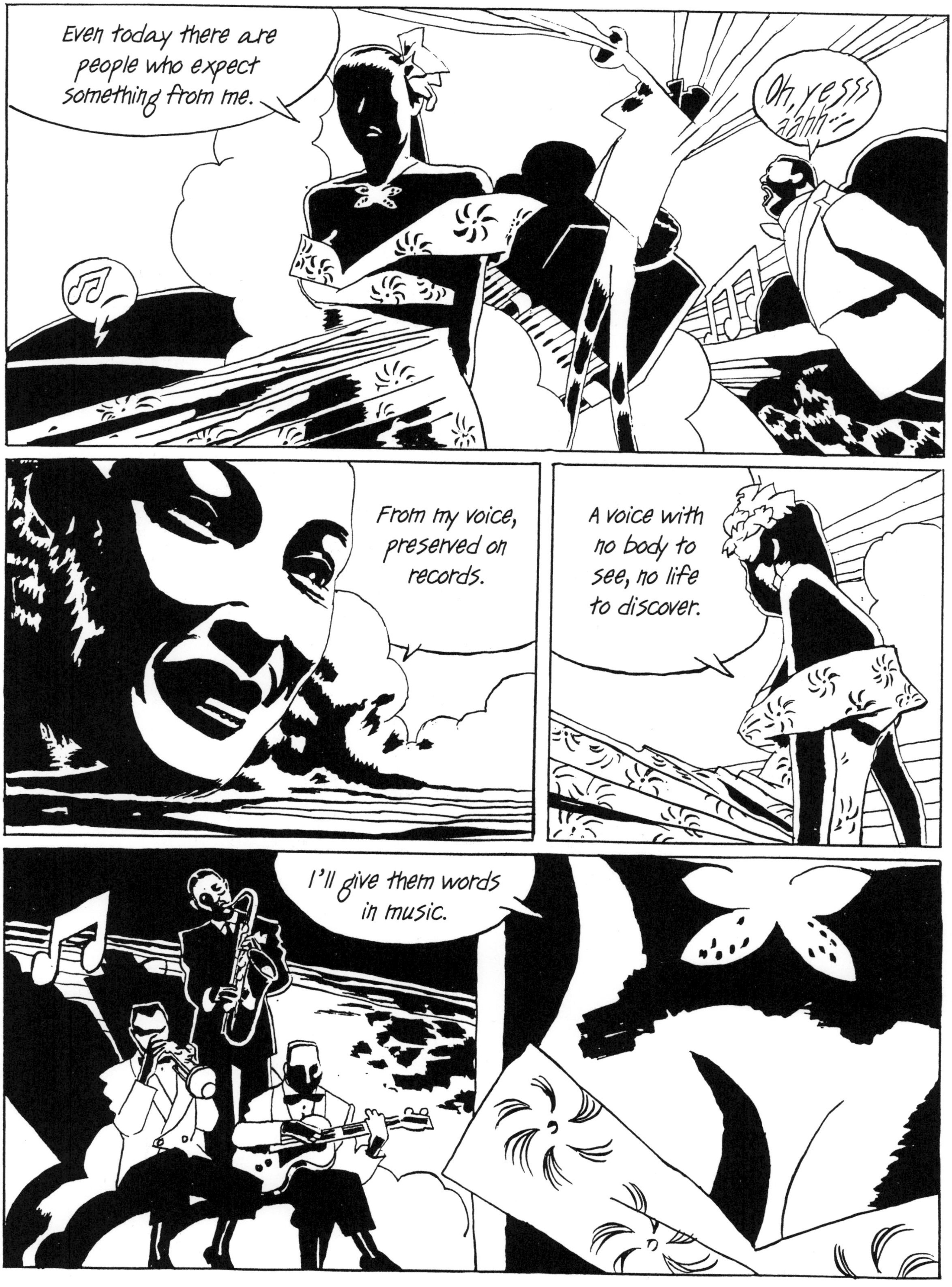
Even today there are people who expect something from me.
Oh, yesss aahh…
From my voice, preserved on records.
A voice with no body to see, no life to discover.
I'll give them words in music.

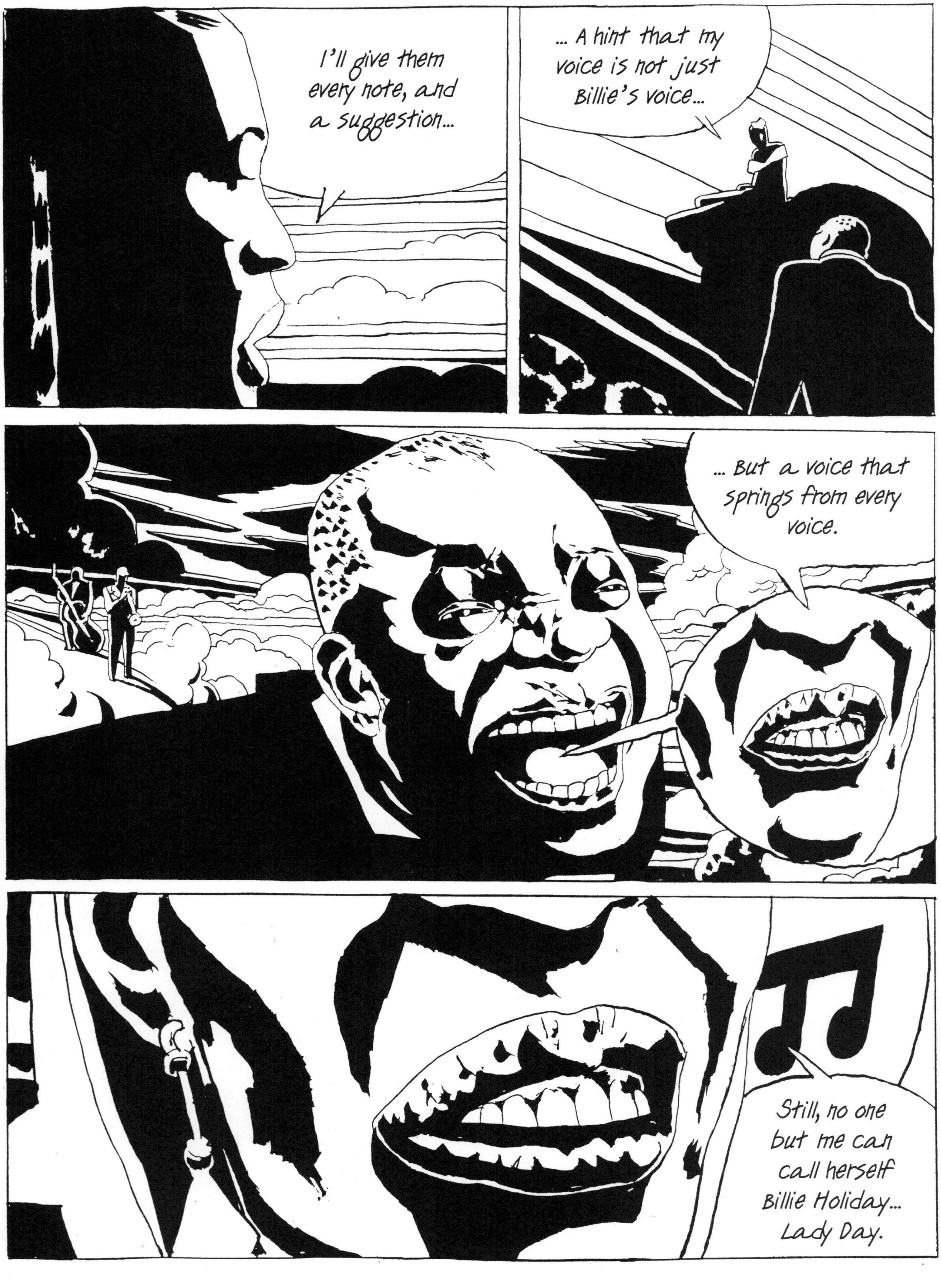
I'll give them every note, and a suggestion...
... A hint that my voice is not just Billie's voice...
... But a voice that springs from every voice.
Still, no one but me can call herself Billie Holiday... Lady Day.

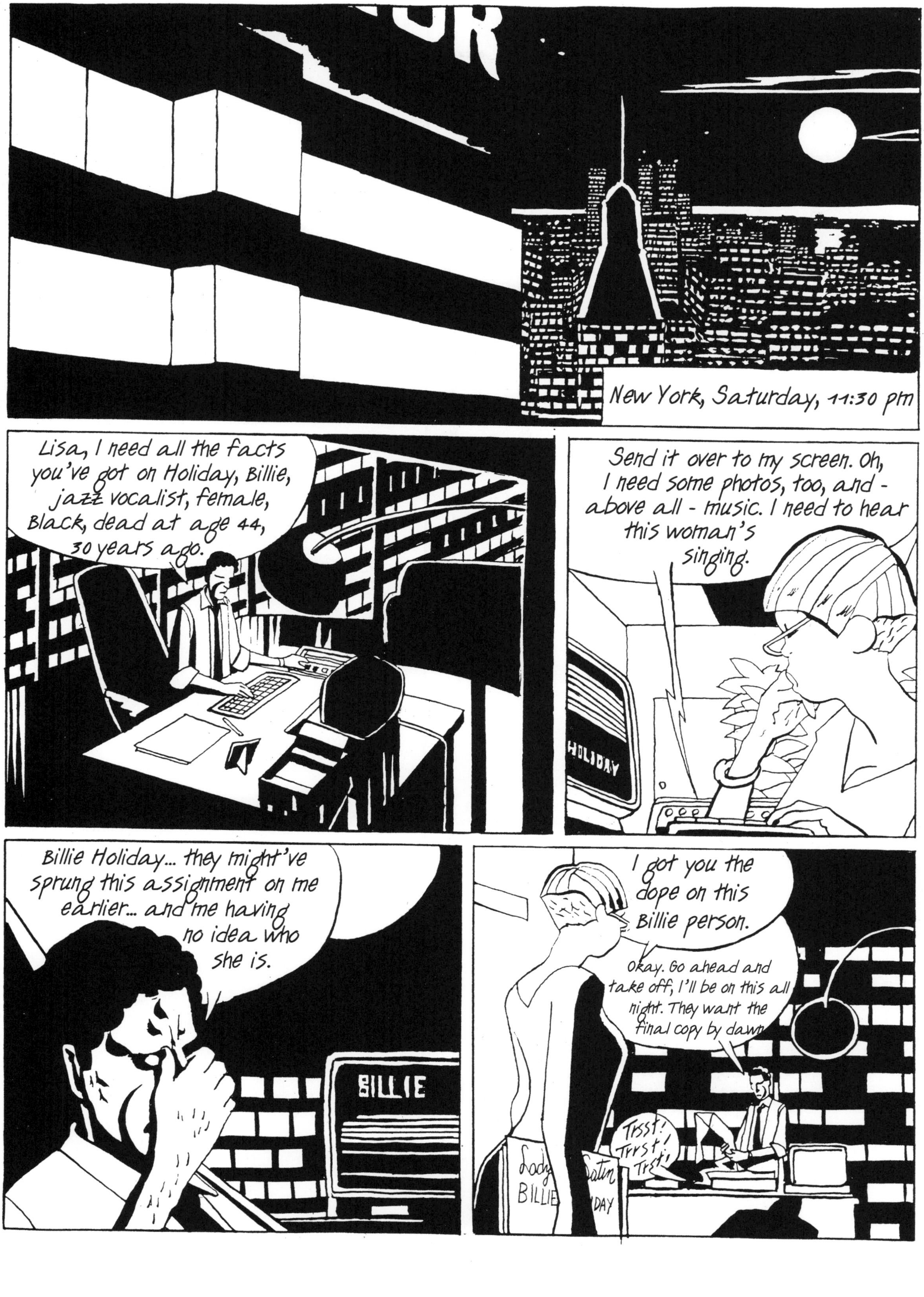
New York, Saturday, 11:30 pm
Lisa, I need all the facts you've got on Holiday, Billie, jazz vocalist, female, Black, dead at age 44, 30 years ago.
Send it over to my screen. Oh, I need some photos, too, and - above all - music. I need to hear this woman's singing.
HOLIDAY
Billie Holiday... they might've sprung this assignment on me earlier... and me having no idea who she is.
BILLIE
I got you the dope on this Billie person.
Okay. Go ahead and take off, I'll be on this all night. They want the final copy by dawn.
Trsst! Trrst! Trst!
BILLIE
DAY

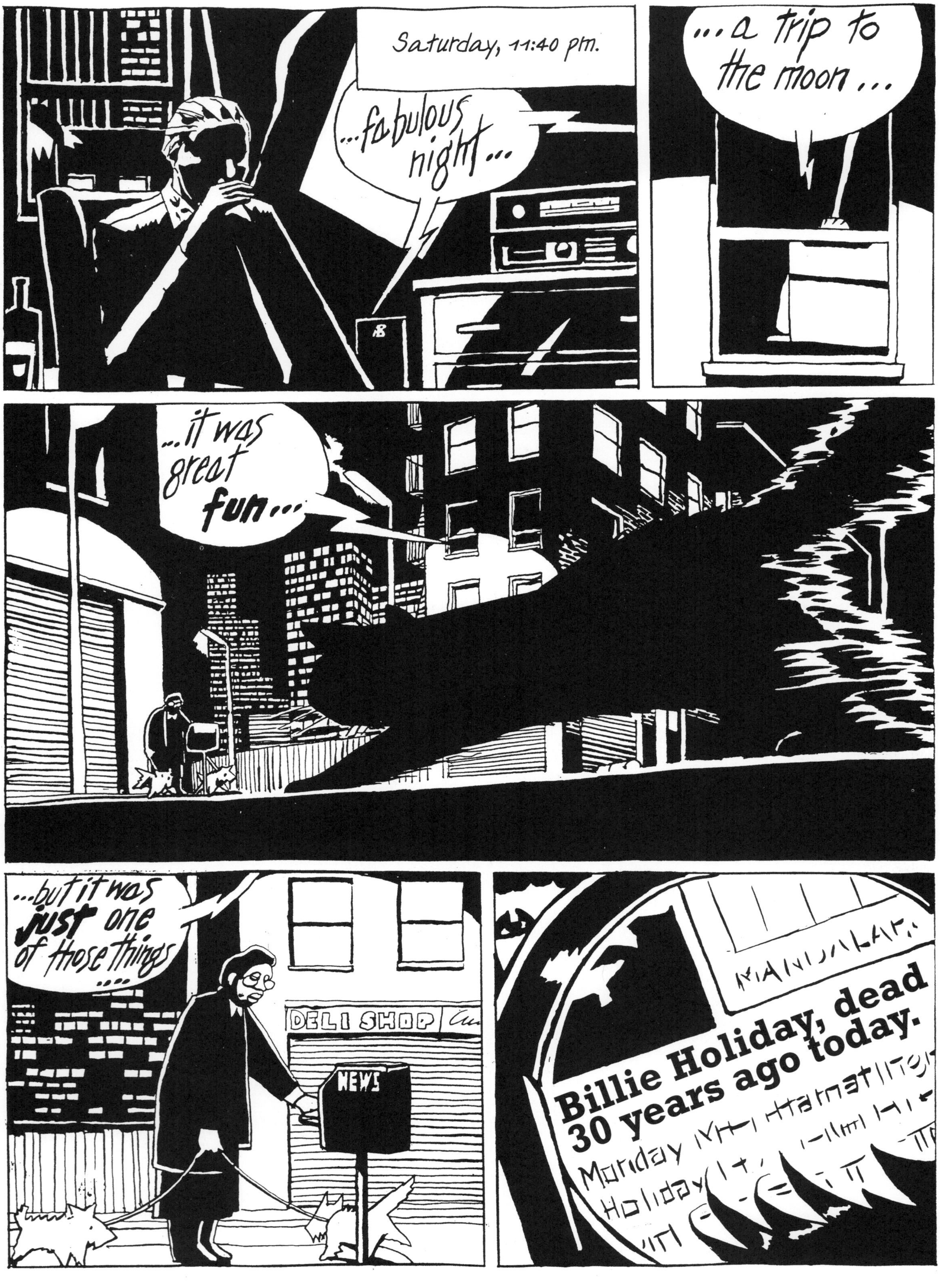
Saturday, 11:40 pm.
...fabulous night...
...a trip to the moon...
...it was great fun...
...but it was just one of those things...
DELI SHOP
NEWS
Billie Holiday, dead 30 years ago today.
Monday
Holiday

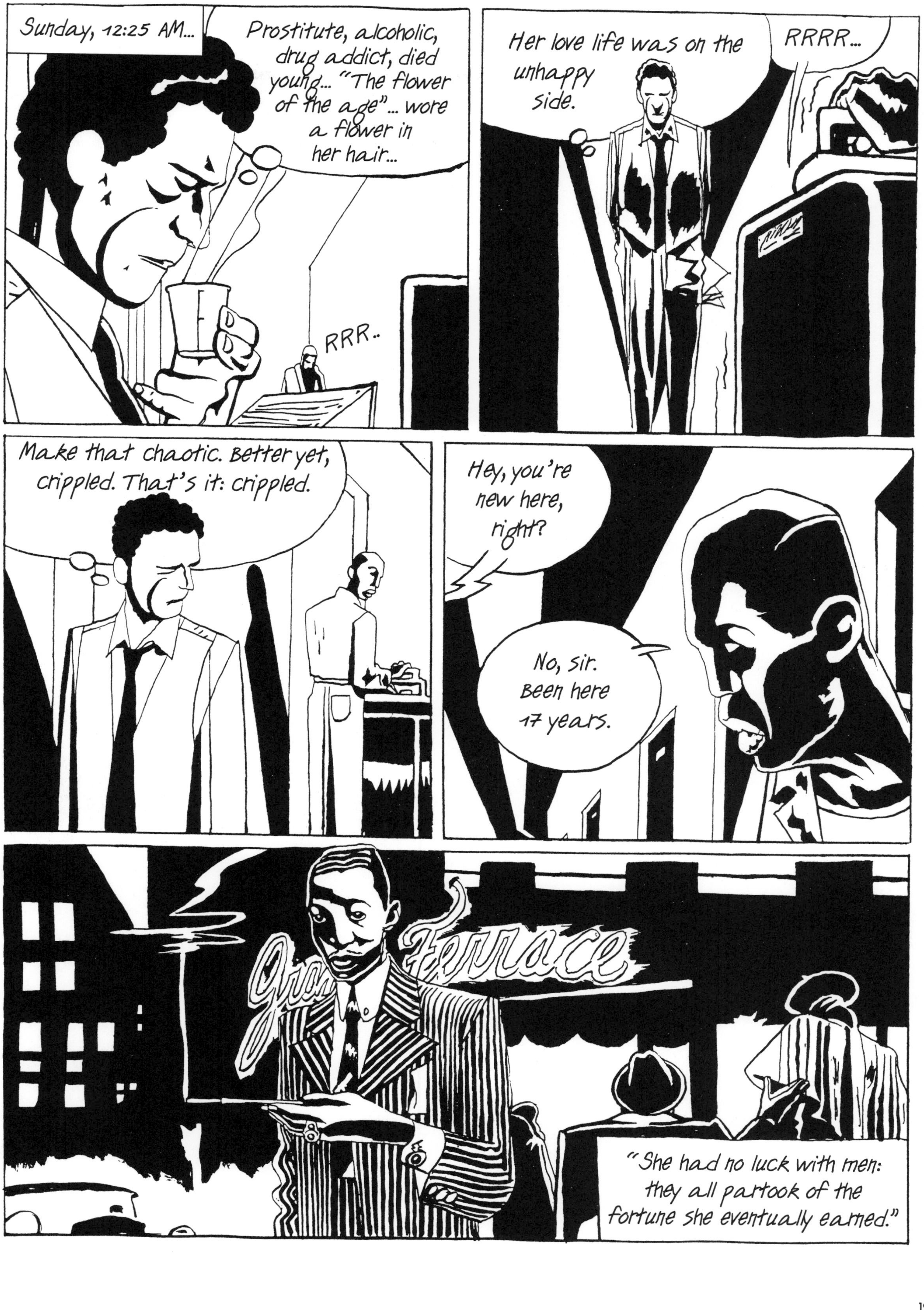
Sunday, 12:25 AM...
Prostitute, alcoholic, drug addict, died young... "The flower of the age"... wore a flower in her hair...
RRR..
Her love life was on the unhappy side.
RRRR...
Make that chaotic. Better yet, crippled. That's it: crippled.
Hey, you're new here, right?
No, sir. Been here 17 years.
"She had no luck with men: they all partook of the fortune she eventually earned."

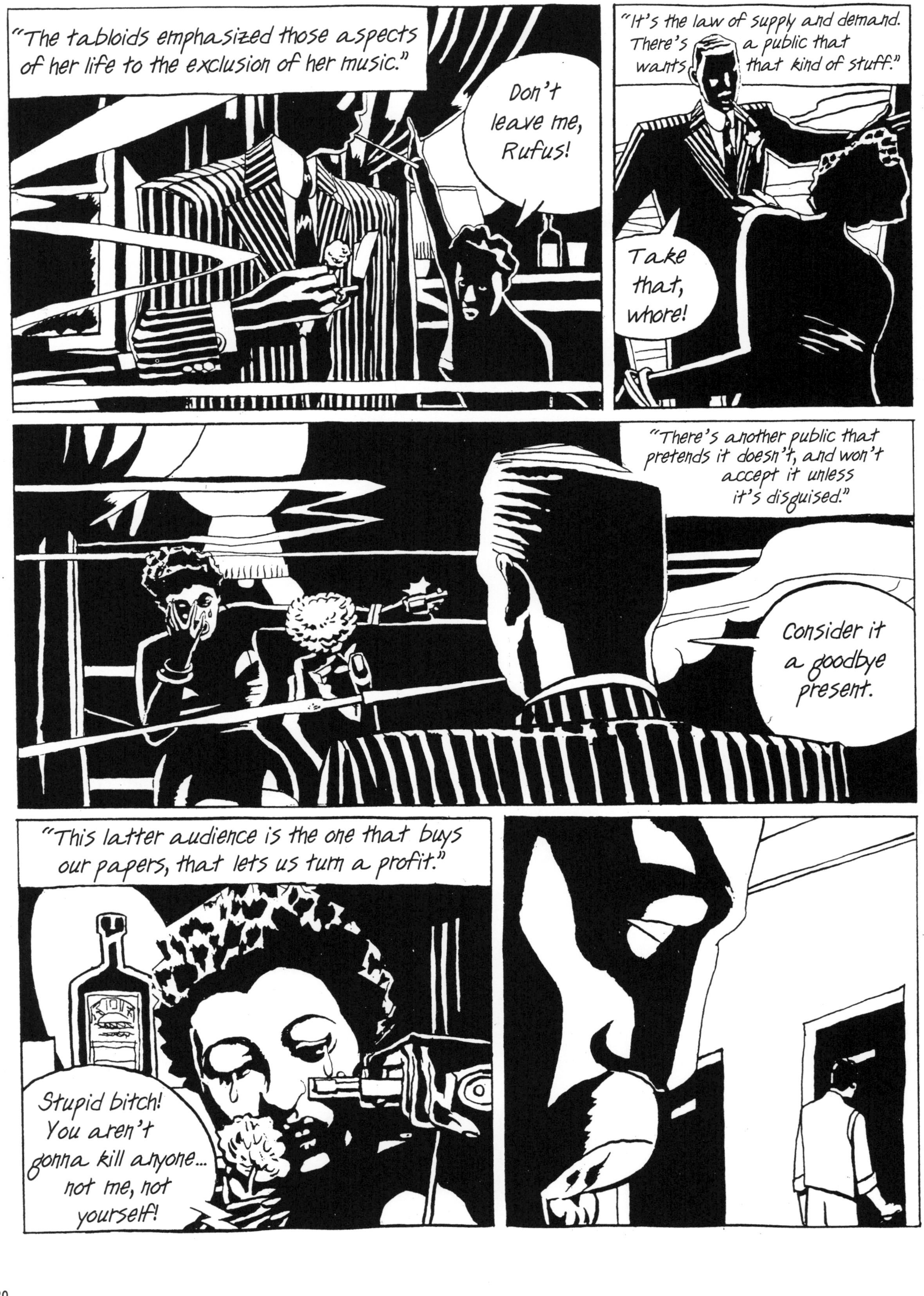
"The tabloids emphasized those aspects of her life to the exclusion of her music."
Don't leave me, Rufus!
"It's the law of supply and demand. There's a public that wants that kind of stuff."
Take that, whore!
"There's another public that pretends it doesn't, and won't accept it unless it's disguised."
Consider it a goodbye present.
"This latter audience is the one that buys our papers, that lets us turn a profit."
Stupid bitch! You aren't gonna kill anyone... not me, not yourself!

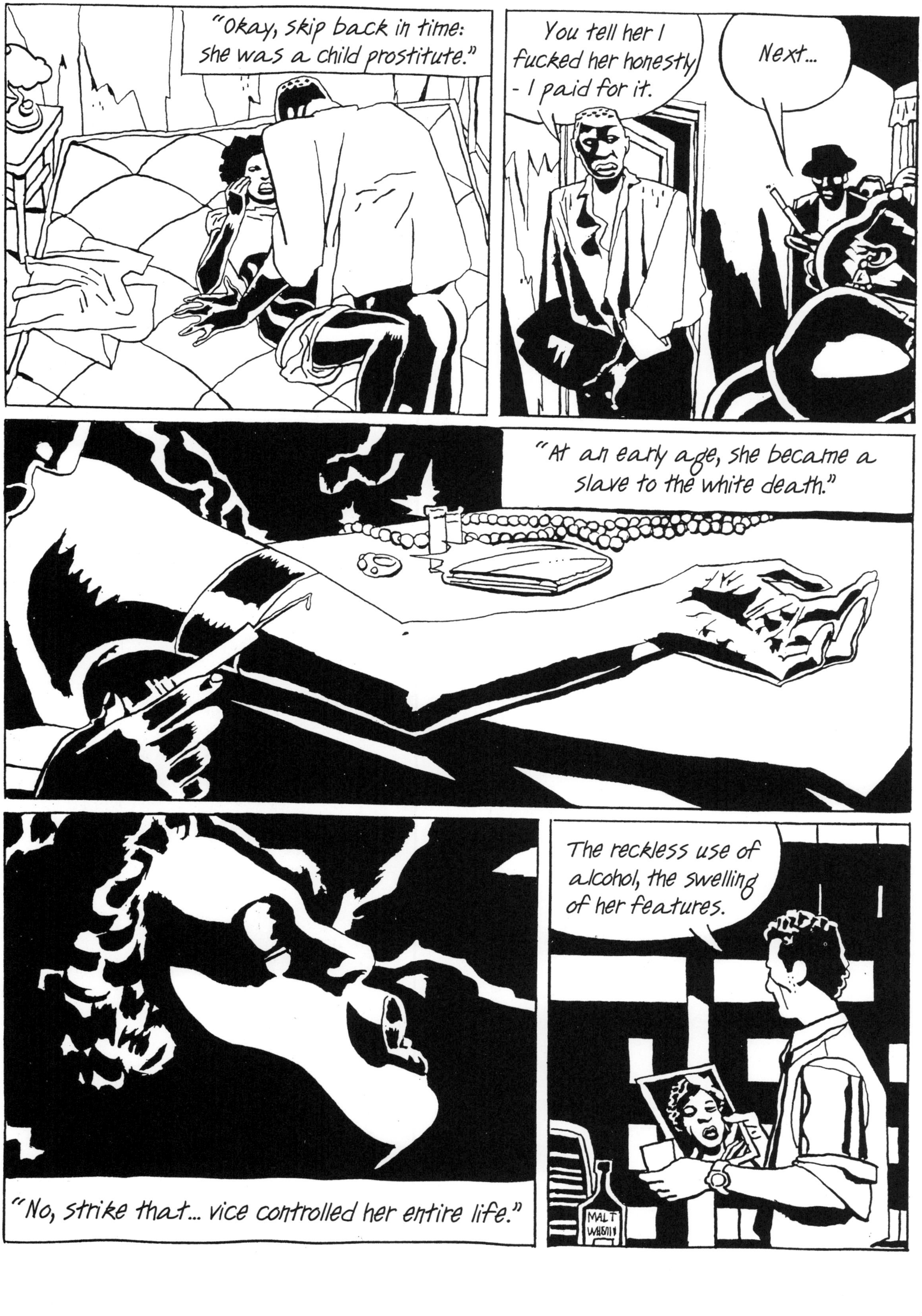
"Okay, skip back in time: she was a child prostitute."
You tell her I fucked her honestly - I paid for it.
Next...
"At an early age, she became a slave to the white death."
"No, strike that... vice controlled her entire life."
The reckless use of alcohol, the swelling of her features.
MALT WHSKY

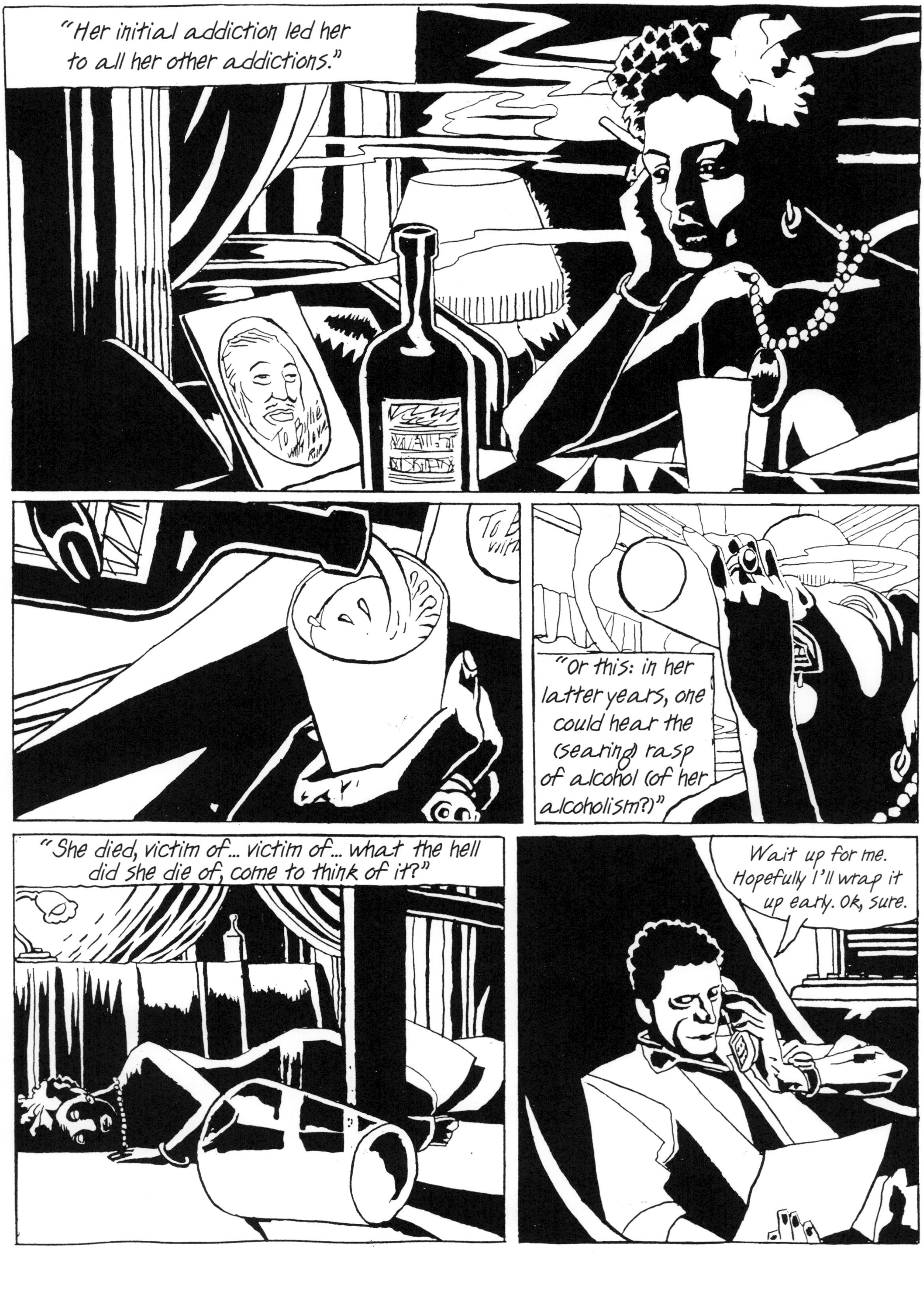
"Her initial addiction led her to all her other addictions."
"Or this: in her latter years, one could hear the (searing) rasp of alcohol (of her alcoholism?)"
"She died, victim of... victim of... what the hell did she die of, come to think of it?"
Wait up for me. Hopefully I'll wrap it up early. Ok, sure.

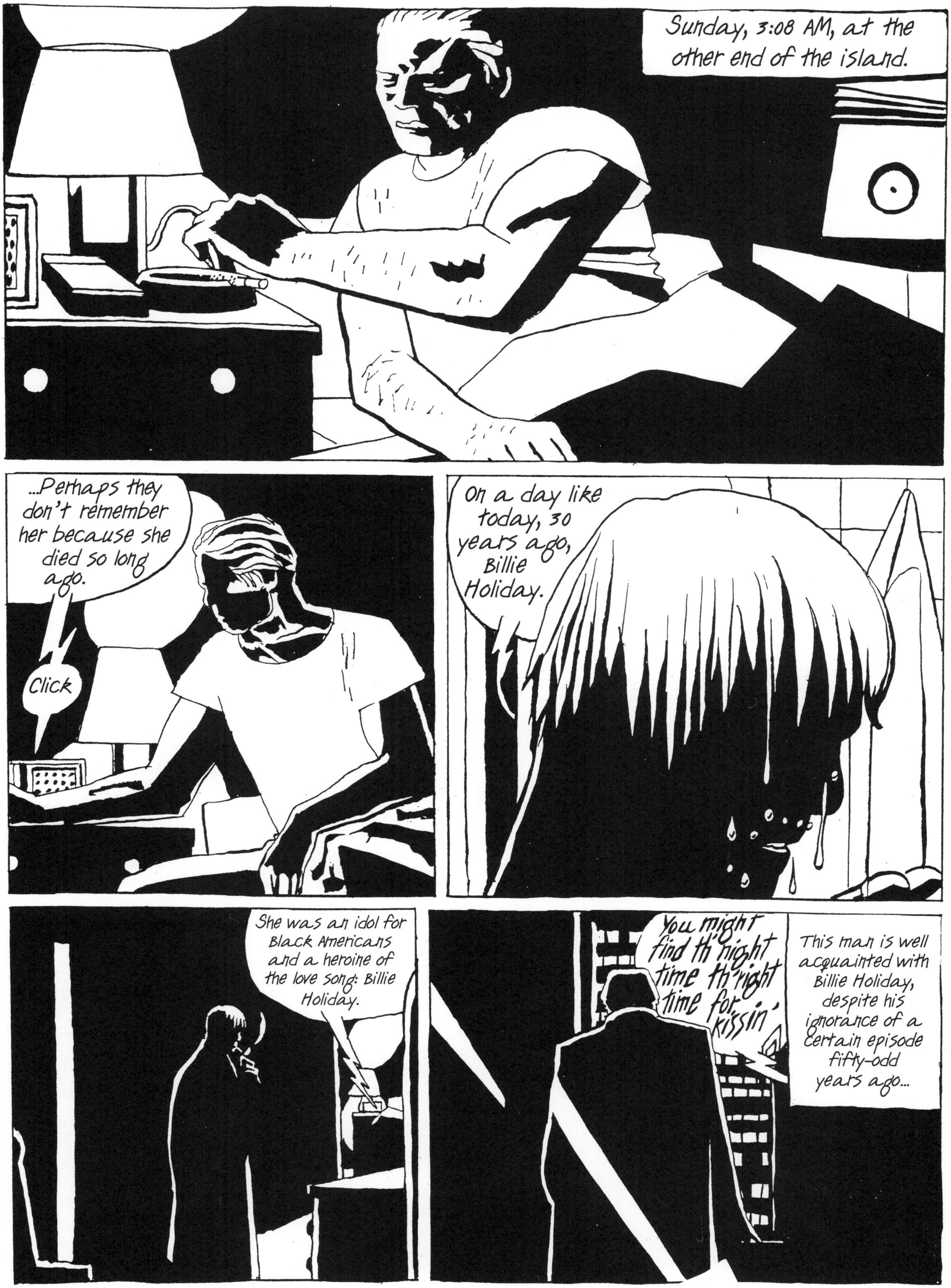

Sunday, 3:08 AM, at the other end of the island.
...Perhaps they don't remember her because she died so long ago.
Click
On a day like today, 30 years ago, Billie Holiday.
She was an idol for Black Americans and a heroine of the love song: Billie Holiday.
You might find th night time th'right time for kissin'
This man is well acquainted with Billie Holiday, despite his ignorance of a certain episode fifty-odd years ago...

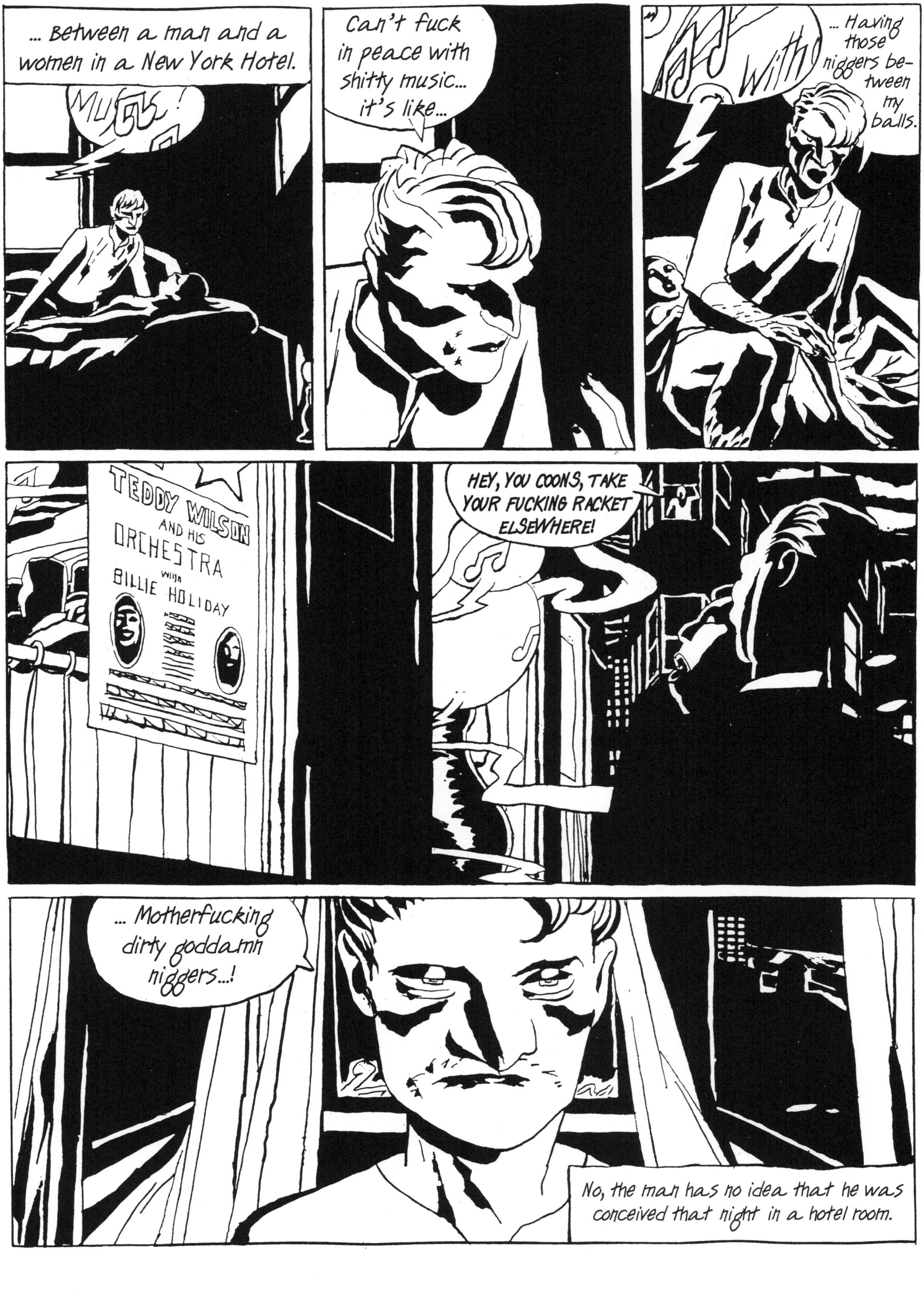
... Between a man and a women in a New York Hotel.
MUSIC!
Can't fuck in peace with shitty music... it's like...
with
... Having those niggers be-tween my balls.
TEDDY WILSON AND HIS ORCHESTRA WITH BILLIE HOLIDAY
HEY, YOU COONS, TAKE YOUR FUCKING RACKET ELSEWHERE!
... Motherfucking dirty goddamn niggers...!
No, the man has no idea that he was conceived that night in a hotel room.

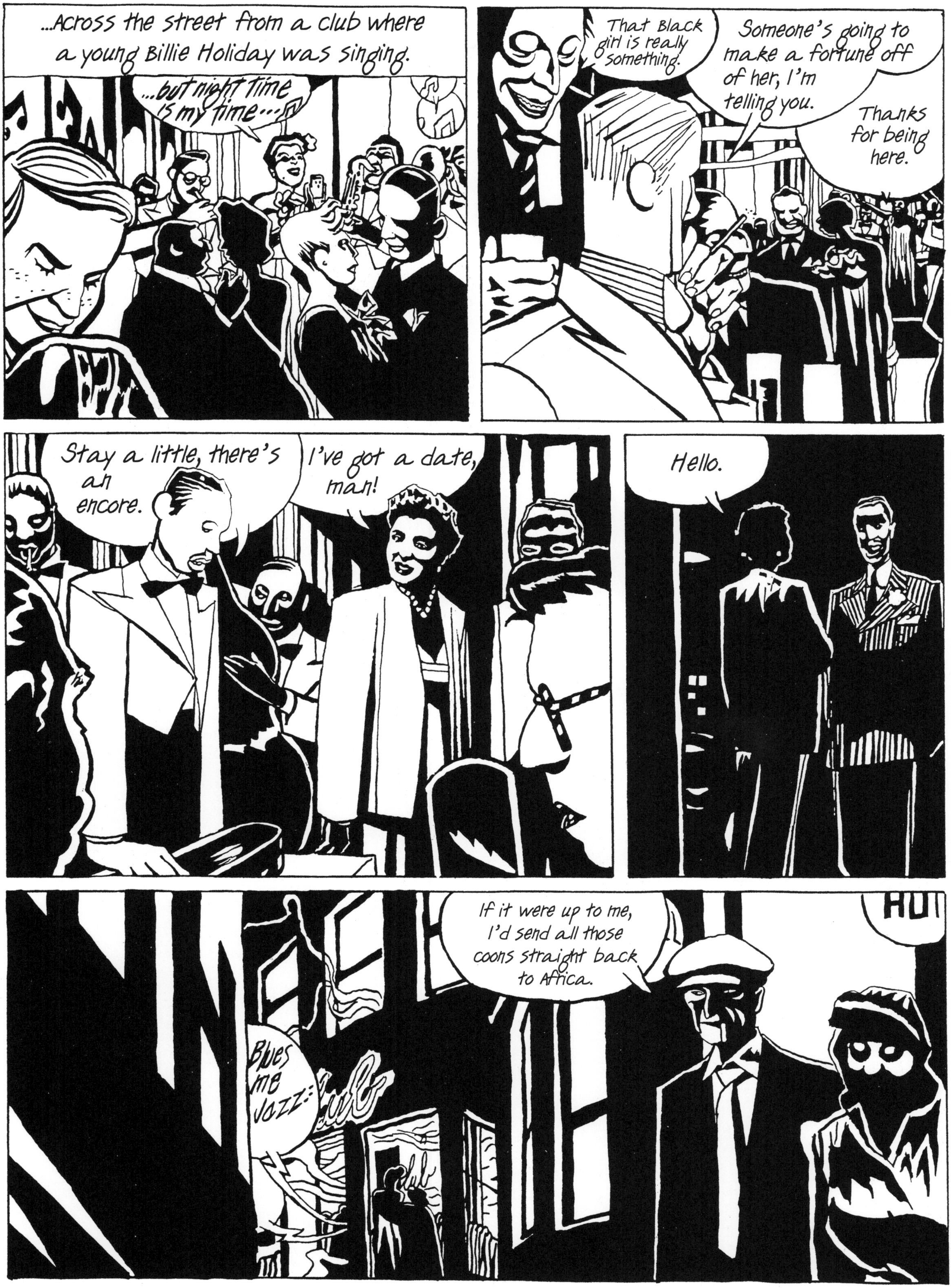
...Across the street from a club where a young Billie Holiday was singing.
...but night time is my time...
That Black girl is really something.
Someone's going to make a fortune off of her, I'm telling you.
Thanks for being here.
Stay a little, there's an encore.
I've got a date, man!
Hello.
If it were up to me, I'd send all those coons straight back to Africa.
Blues me Jazz

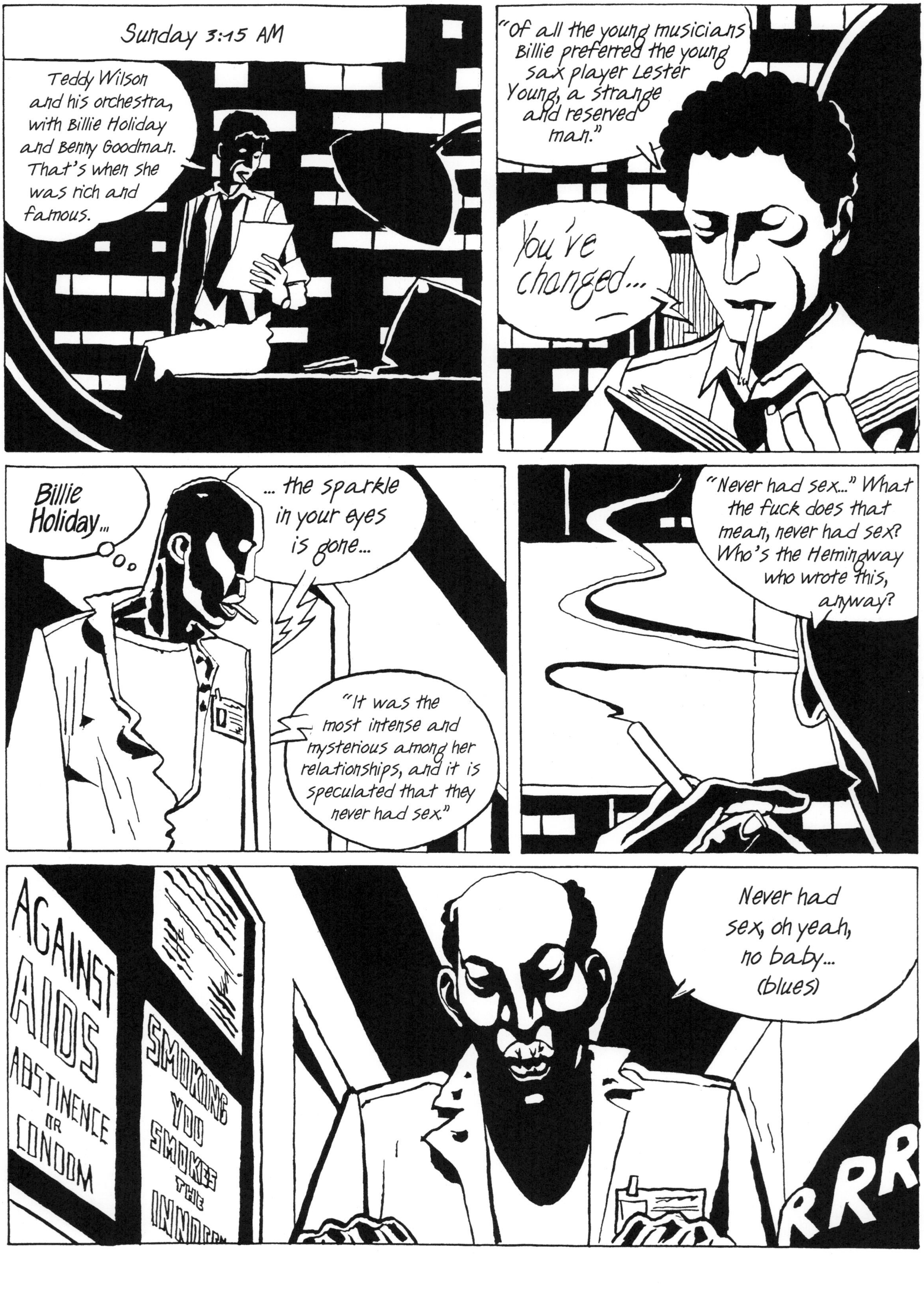

Sunday 3:15 AM
Teddy Wilson and his orchestra, with Billie Holiday and Benny Goodman. That's when she was rich and famous.
"Of all the young musicians Billie preferred the young sax player Lester Young, a strange and reserved man."
You've changed...
Billie Holiday...
... the sparkle in your eyes is gone...
"It was the most intense and mysterious among her relationships, and it is speculated that they never had sex."
"Never had sex..." What the fuck does that mean, never had sex? Who's the Hemingway who wrote this, anyway?
AGAINST AIDS ABSTINENCE OR CONDOM
SMOKING YOU SMOKES THE
Never had sex, oh yeah, no baby... (blues)
RRR

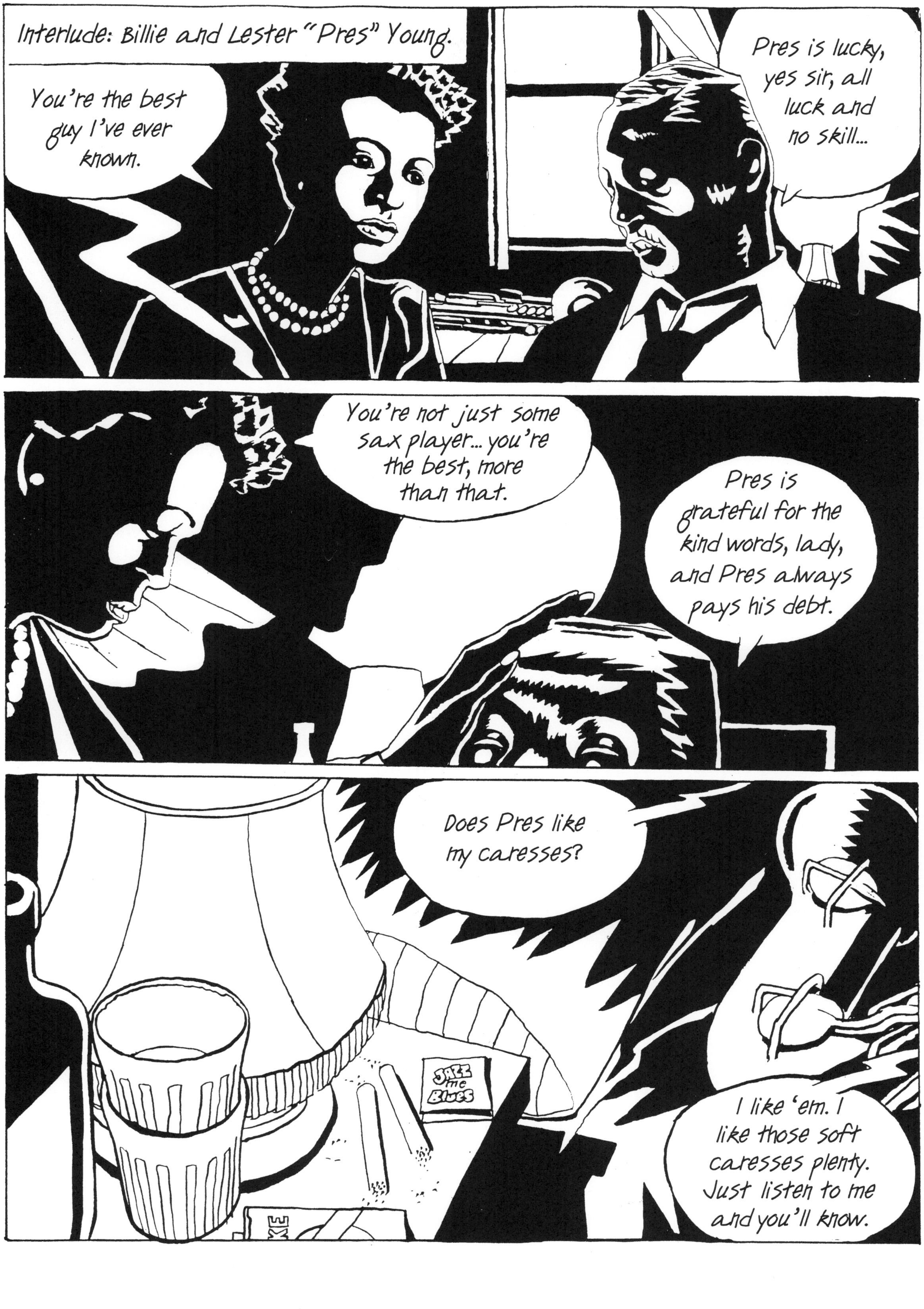
Interlude: Billie and Lester "Pres" Young.
You're the best guy I've ever known.
Pres is lucky, yes sir, all luck and no skill...
You're not just some sax player... you're the best, more than that.
Pres is grateful for the kind words, lady, and Pres always pays his debt.
Does Pres like my caresses?
JAZZ me BLUES
I like 'em. I like those soft caresses plenty. Just listen to me and you'll know.

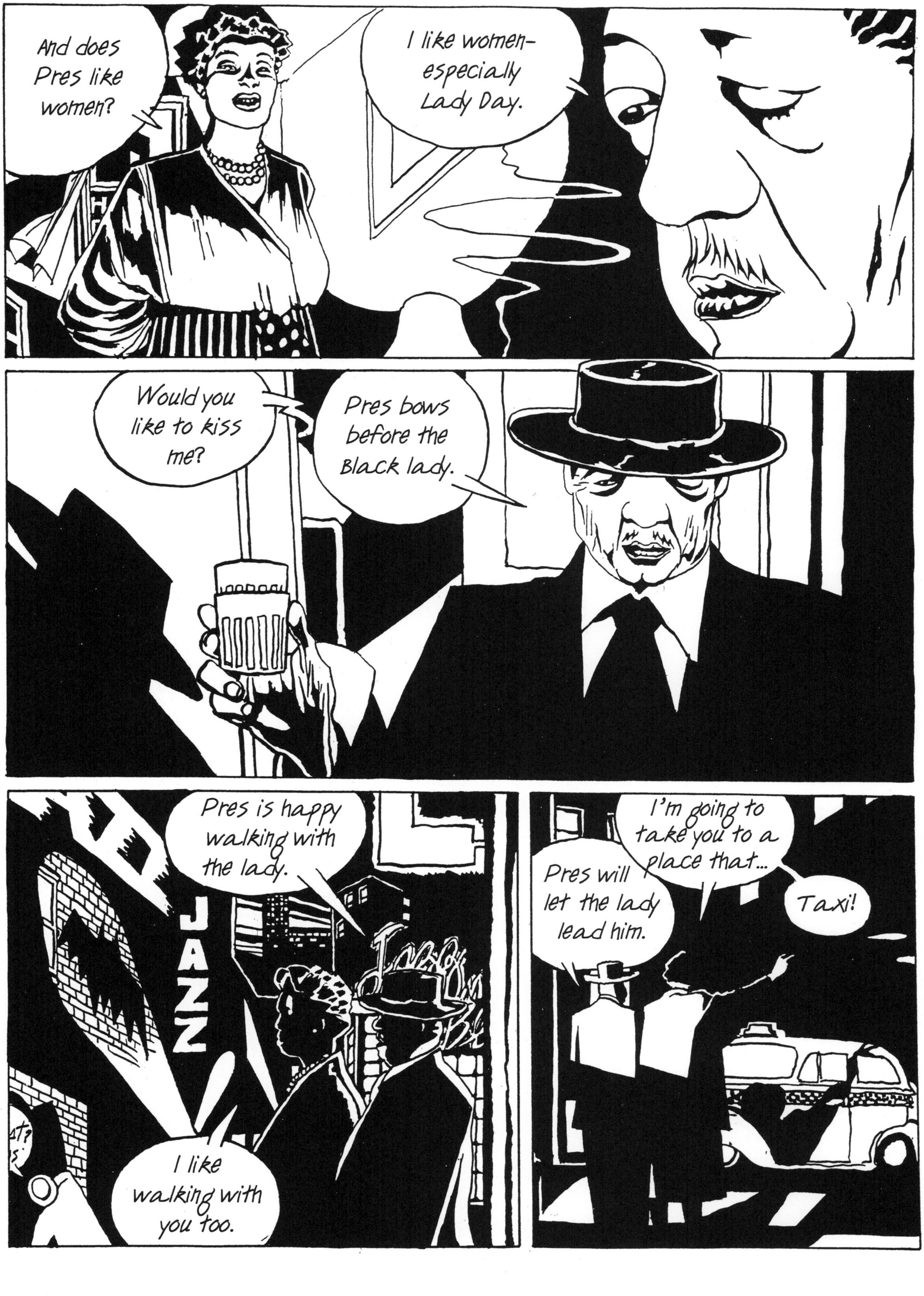
And does Pres like women?
I like women- especially Lady Day.
Would you like to kiss me?
Pres bows before the Black lady.
Pres is happy walking with the lady.
I like walking with you too.
Pres will let the lady lead him.
I'm going to take you to a place that...
Taxi!
JAZZ

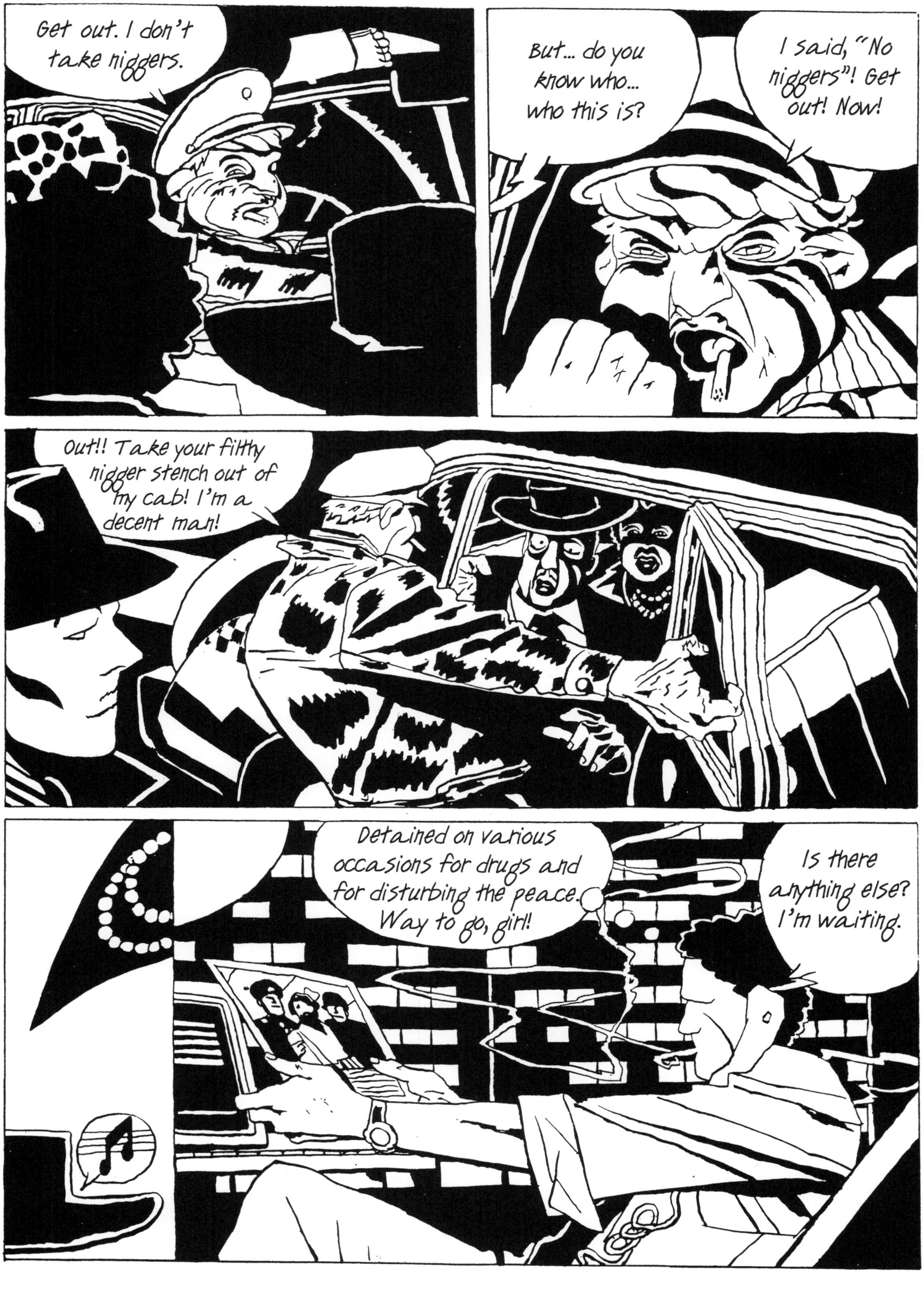
Get out. I don't take niggers.
But... do you know who... who this is?
I said, "No niggers"! Get out! Now!
Out!! Take your filthy nigger stench out of my cab! I'm a decent man!
Detained on various occasions for drugs and for disturbing the peace. Way to go, girl!
Is there anything else? I'm waiting.

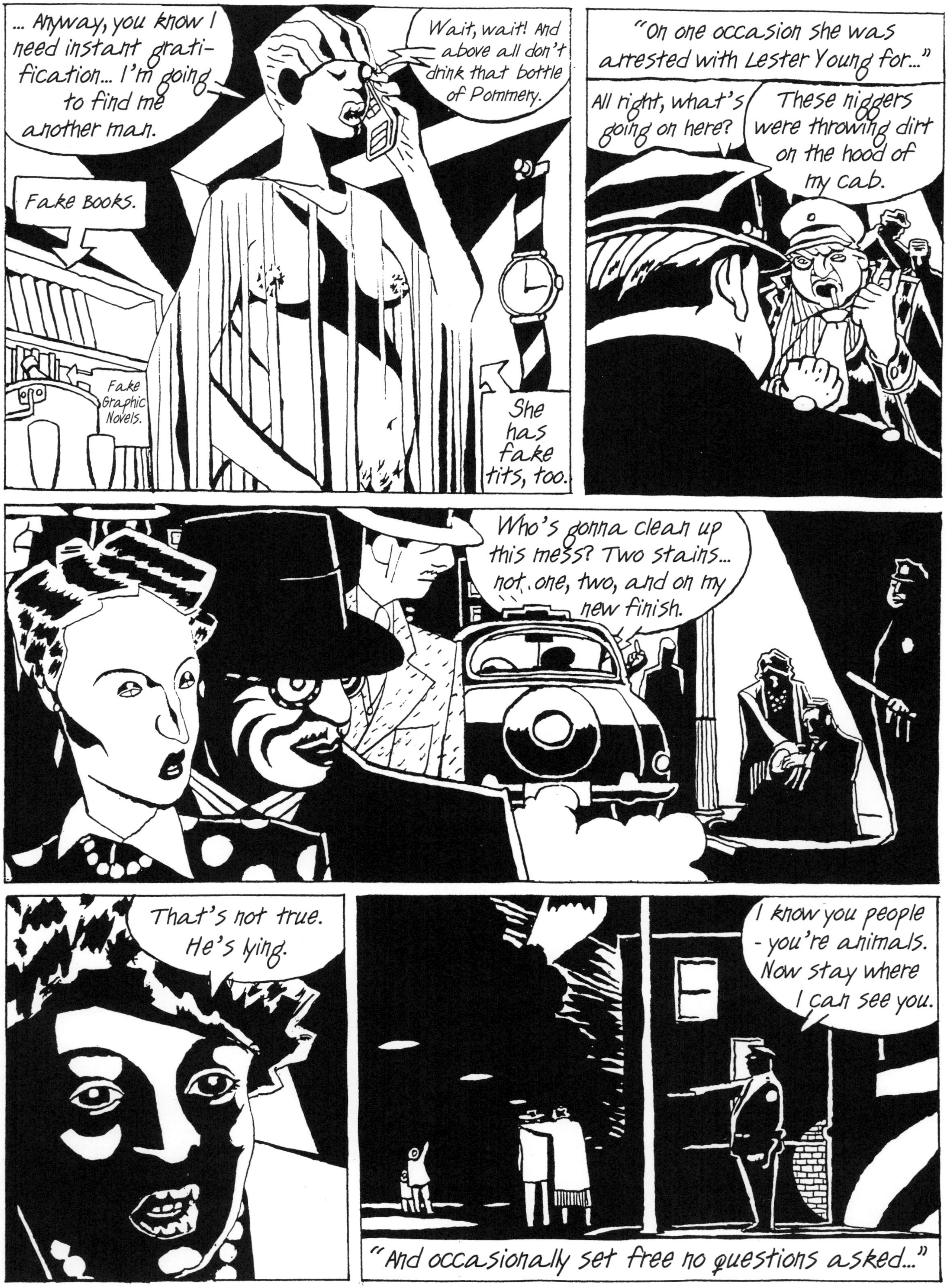

... Anyway, you know I need instant gratification... I'm going to find me another man.
Wait, wait! And above all don't drink that bottle of Pommery.
Fake Books.
Fake Graphic Novels.
She has fake tits, too.
"On one occasion she was arrested with Lester Young for..."
All right, what's going on here?
These niggers were throwing dirt on the hood of my cab.
Who's gonna clean up this mess? Two stains... not one, two, and on my new finish.
That's not true. He's lying.
I know you people - you're animals. Now stay where I can see you.
"And occasionally set free no questions asked..."

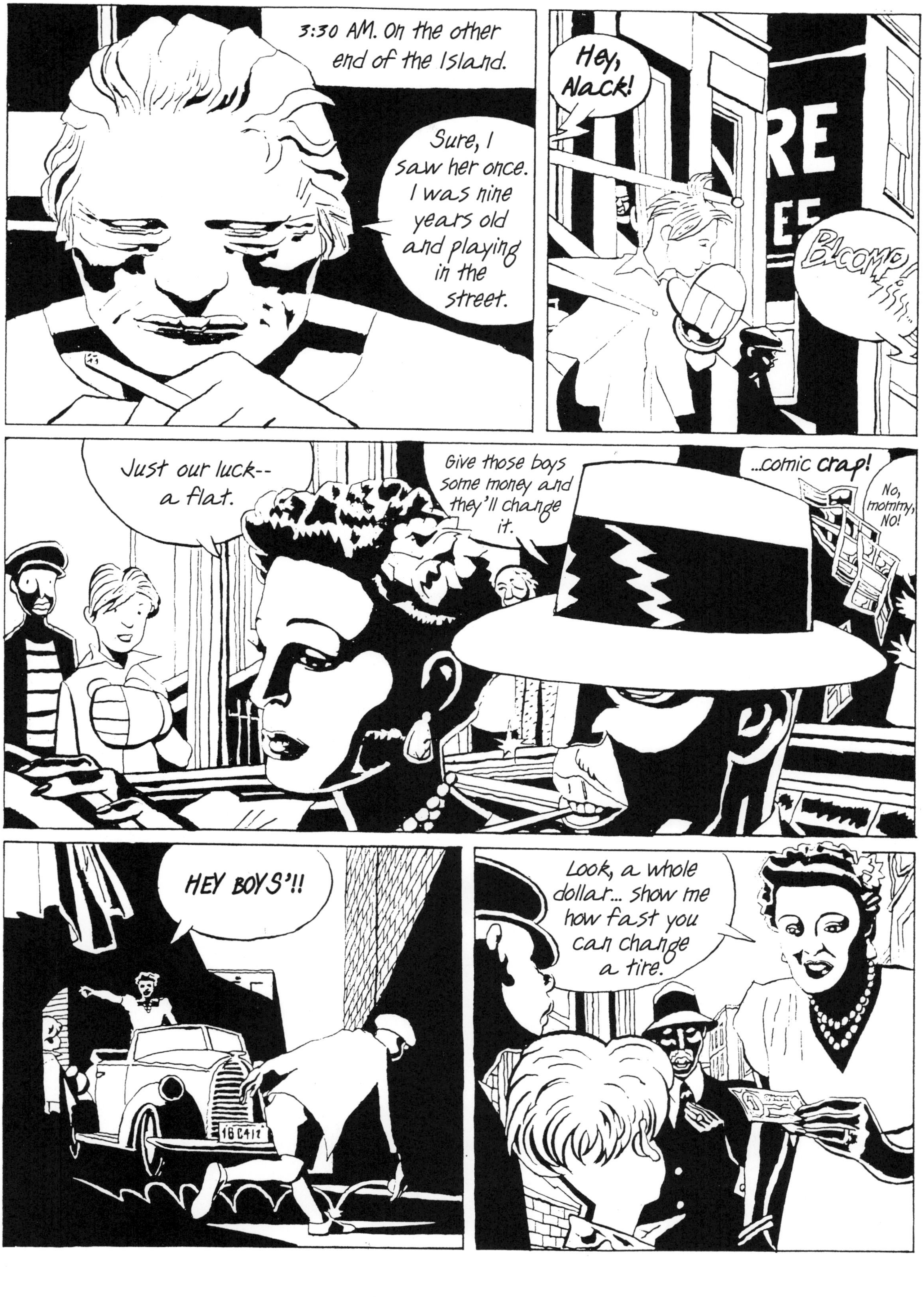
3:30 AM. On the other end of the Island.
Sure, I saw her once. I was nine years old and playing in the street.
Hey, Alack!
BLOOMP!!
RE
ES
Just our luck-- a flat.
Give those boys some money and they'll change it.
...comic crap!
No, mommy, NO!
HEY BOYS'!!
Look, a whole dollar... show me how fast you can change a tire.

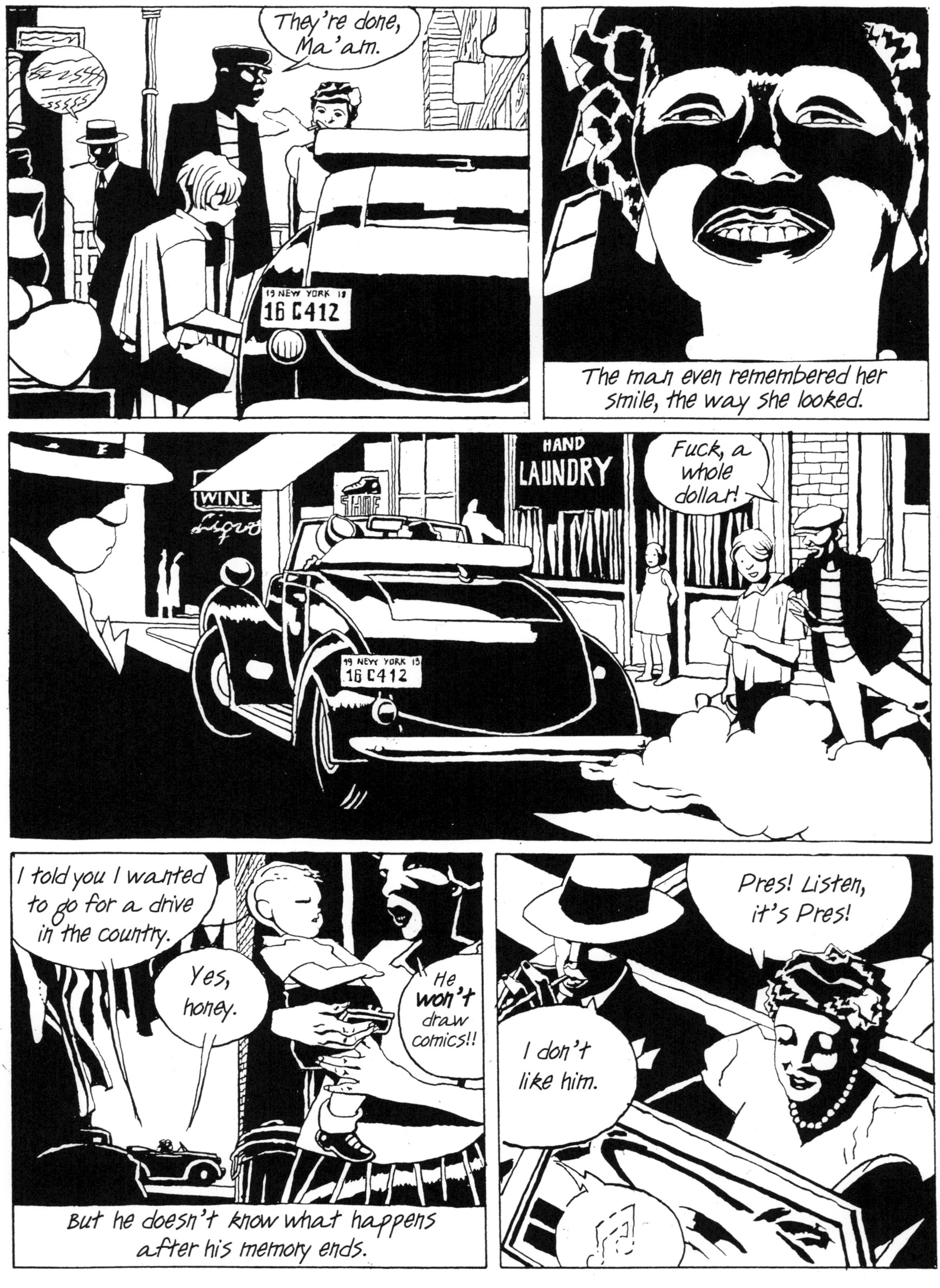
They're done, Ma'am.
19 NEW YORK 19
16 C412
The man even remembered her smile, the way she looked.
HAND LAUNDRY
WINE
Liquor
SHOE
Fuck, a whole dollar!
19 NEW YORK 19
16 C412
I told you I wanted to go for a drive in the country.
Yes, honey.
He **won't** draw comics!!
But he doesn't know what happens after his memory ends.
Pres! Listen, it's Pres!
I don't like him.

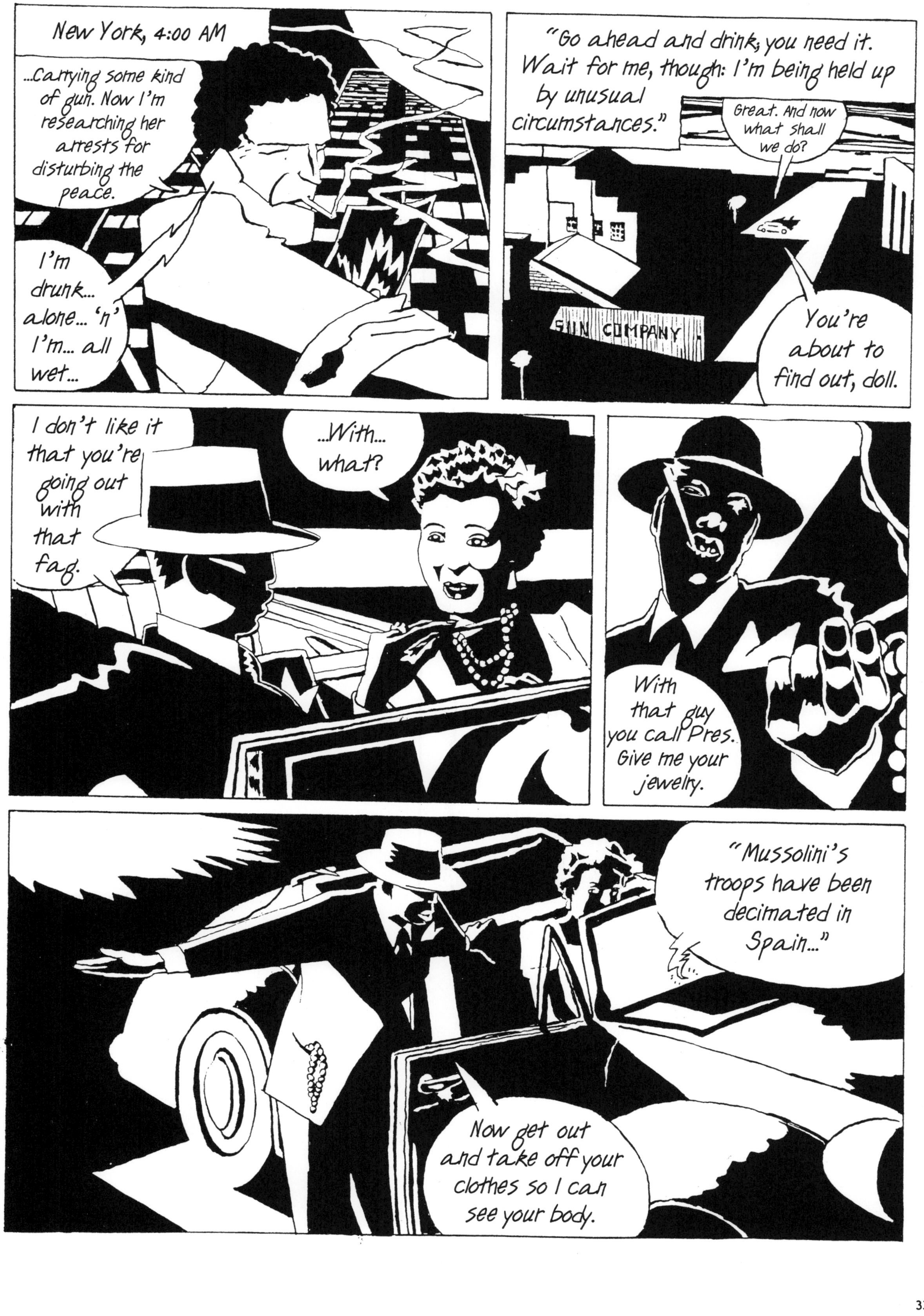
New York, 4:00 AM
...Carrying some kind of gun. Now I'm researching her arrests for disturbing the peace.
I'm drunk... alone... 'n' I'm... all wet...
"Go ahead and drink; you need it. Wait for me, though: I'm being held up by unusual circumstances."
Great. And now what shall we do?
You're about to find out, doll.
GUN COMPANY
I don't like it that you're going out with that fag.
...With... what?
With that guy you call Pres. Give me your jewelry.
"Mussolini's troops have been decimated in Spain..."
Now get out and take off your clothes so I can see your body.

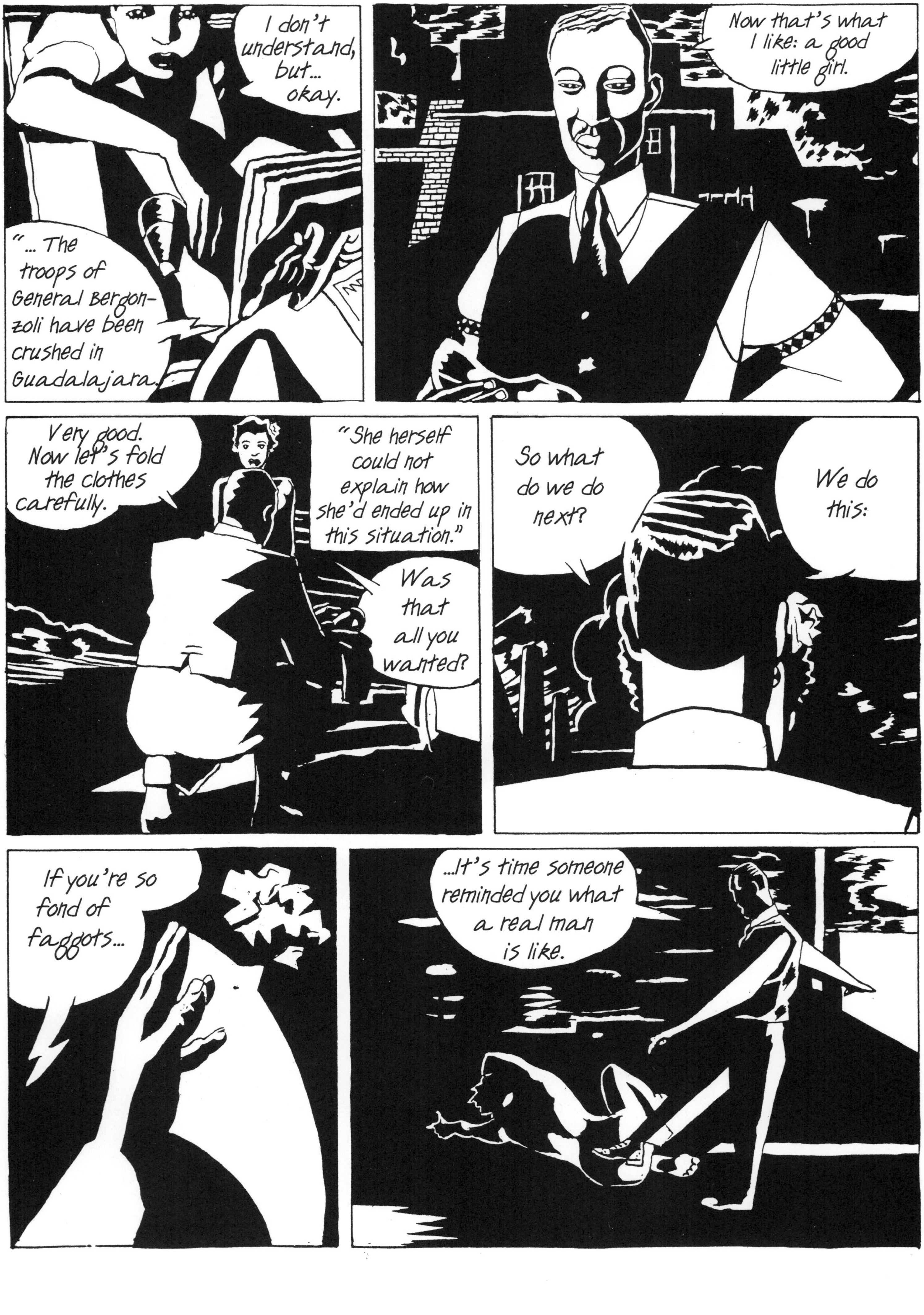
I don't understand, but... okay.
"... The troops of General Bergonzoli have been crushed in Guadalajara.
Now that's what I like: a good little girl.
Very good. Now let's fold the clothes carefully.
"She herself could not explain how she'd ended up in this situation."
Was that all you wanted?
So what do we do next?
We do this:
If you're so fond of faggots...
...It's time someone reminded you what a real man is like.

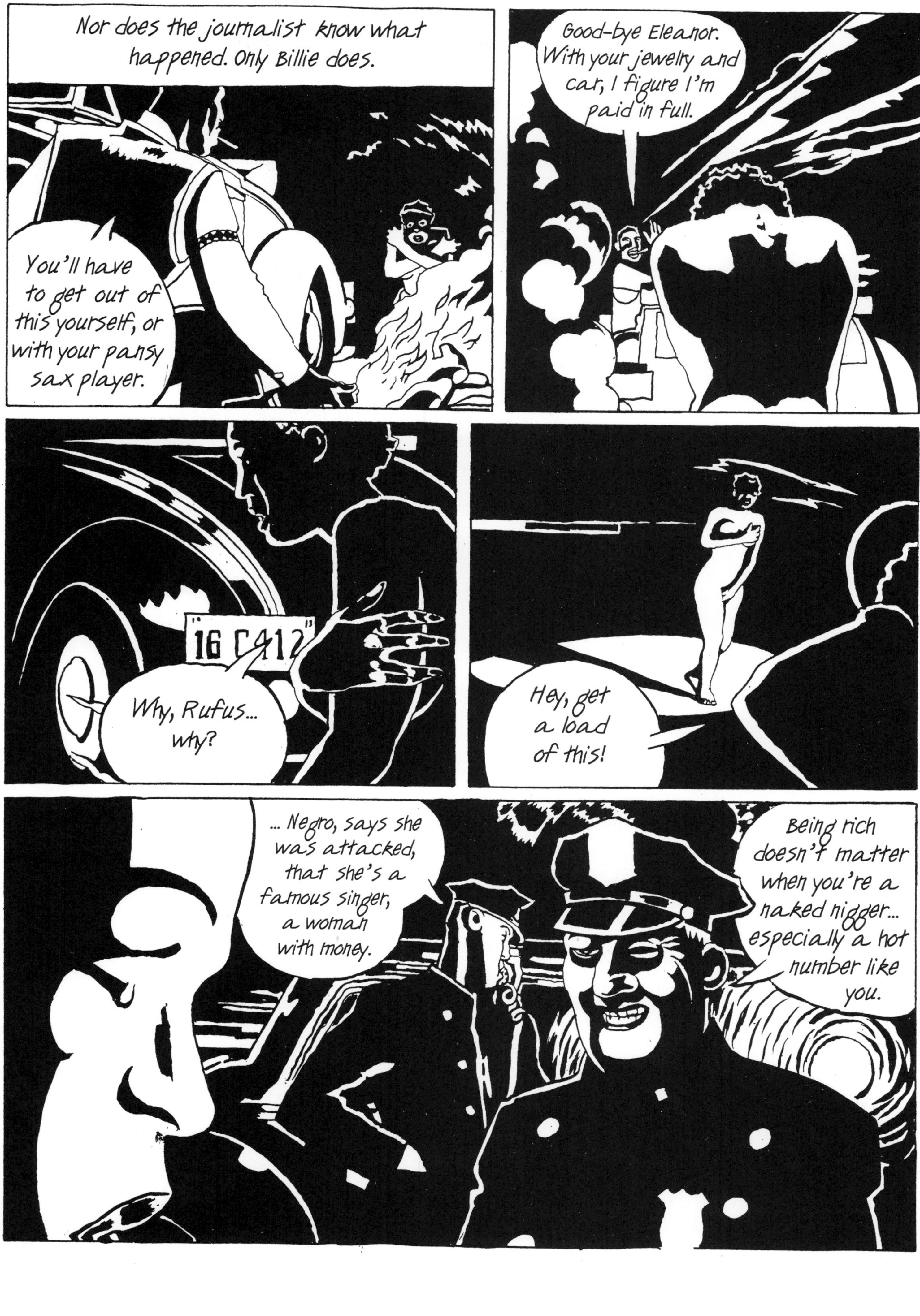
Nor does the journalist know what happened. Only Billie does.
You'll have to get out of this yourself, or with your pansy sax player.
Good-bye Eleanor. With your jewelry and car, I figure I'm paid in full.
16 C412
Why, Rufus... why?
Hey, get a load of this!
... Negro, says she was attacked, that she's a famous singer, a woman with money.
Being rich doesn't matter when you're a naked nigger... especially a hot number like you.

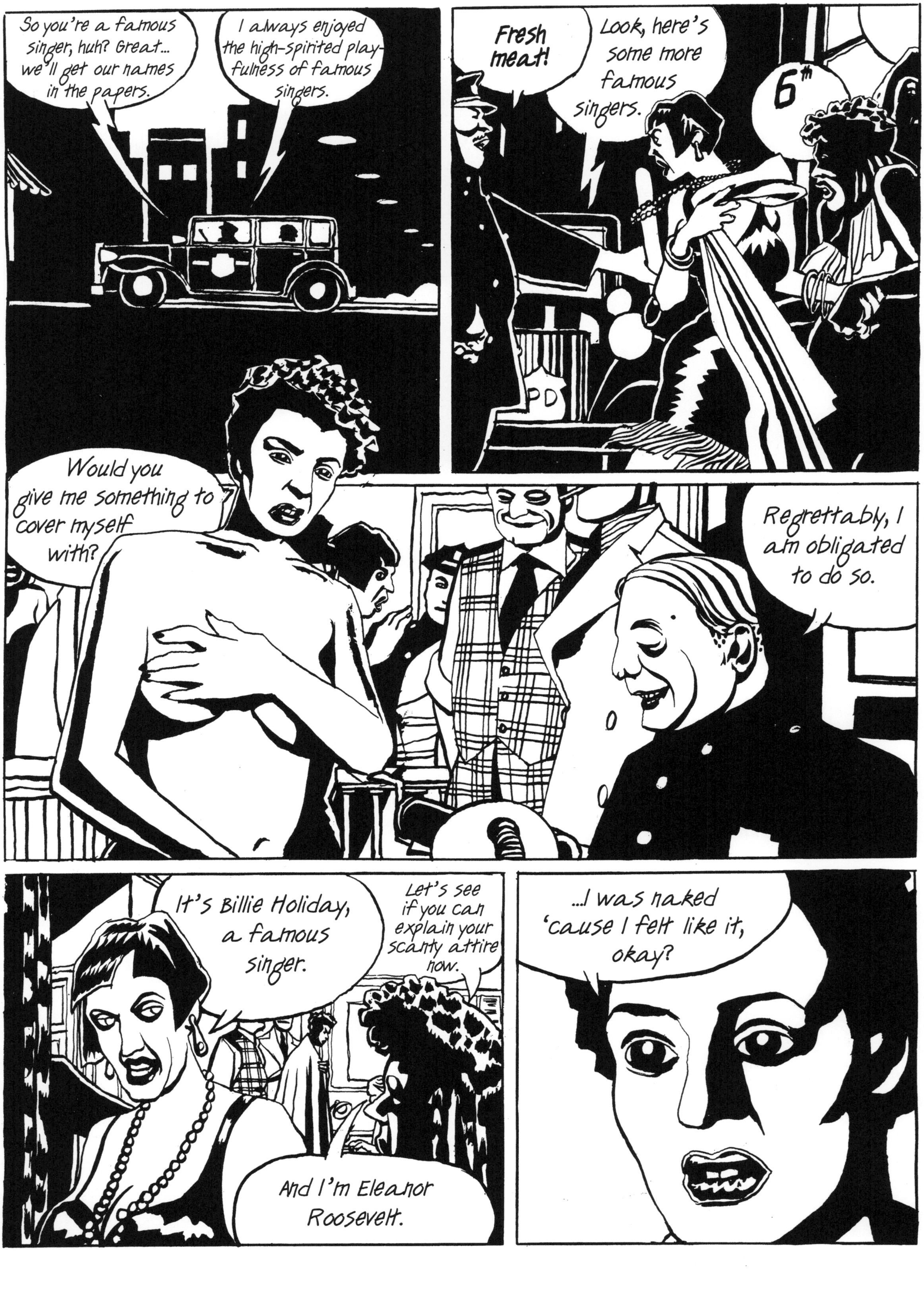
So you're a famous singer, huh? Great... we'll get our names in the papers.
I always enjoyed the high-spirited playfulness of famous singers.
Fresh meat!
Look, here's some more famous singers.
6th
PD
Would you give me something to cover myself with?
Regrettably, I am obligated to do so.
It's Billie Holiday, a famous singer.
Let's see if you can explain your scanty attire now.
And I'm Eleanor Roosevelt.
...I was naked 'cause I felt like it, okay?

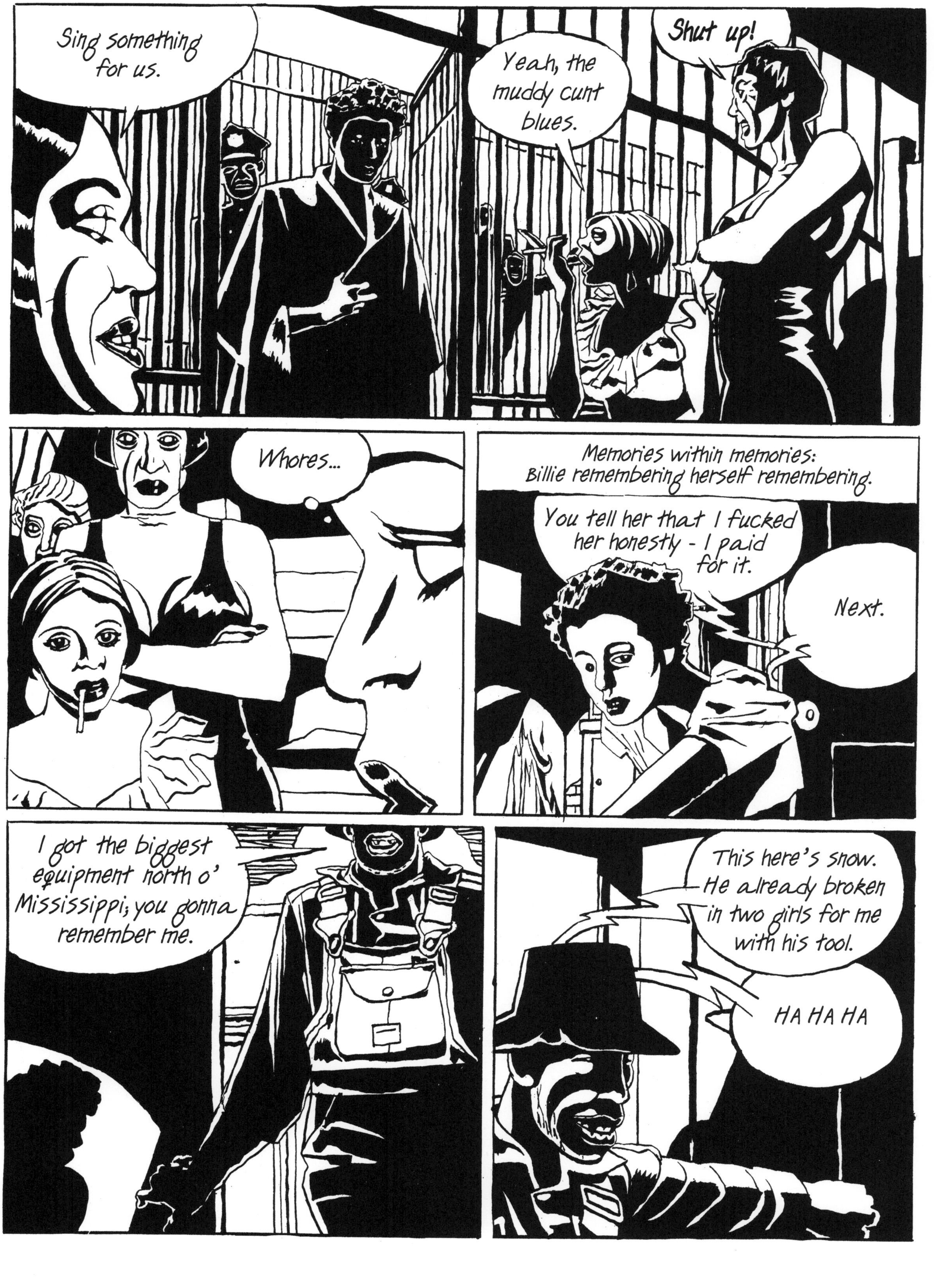
Sing something for us.
Yeah, the muddy cunt blues.
Shut up!
Whores...
Memories within memories: Billie remembering herself remembering.
You tell her that I fucked her honestly - I paid for it.
Next.
I got the biggest equipment north o' Mississippi; you gonna remember me.
This here's snow. He already broken in two girls for me with his tool.
HA HA HA

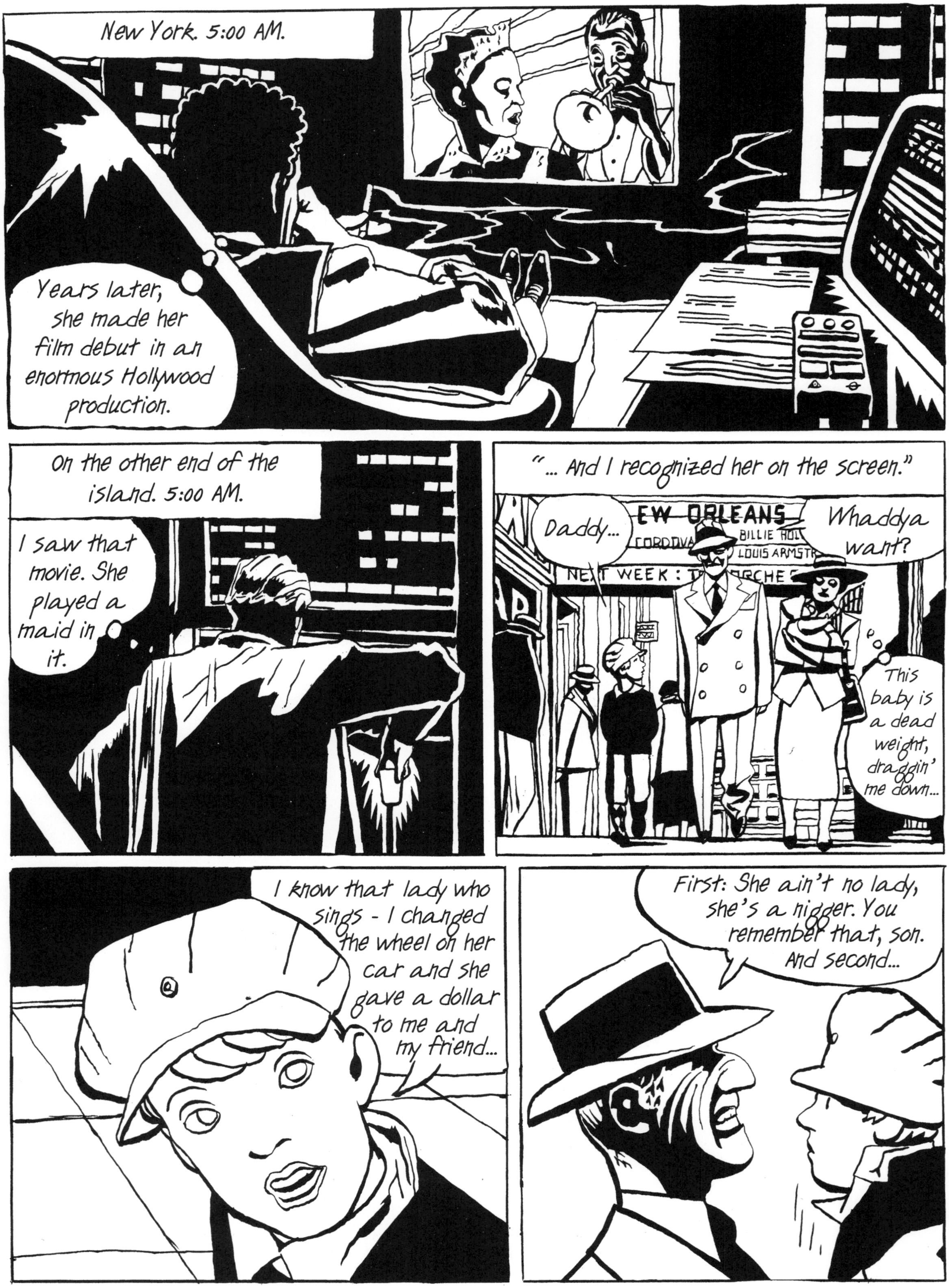
New York. 5:00 AM.
Years later, she made her film debut in an enormous Hollywood production.
On the other end of the island. 5:00 AM.
I saw that movie. She played a maid in it.
"... And I recognized her on the screen."
EW ORLEANS
BILLIE HOL
CORDOVA
LOUIS ARMSTR
NEXT WEEK :
Daddy...
Whaddya want?
This baby is a dead weight, draggin' me down...
I know that lady who sings - I changed the wheel on her car and she gave a dollar to me and my friend...
First: She ain't no lady, she's a nigger. You remember that, son. And second...

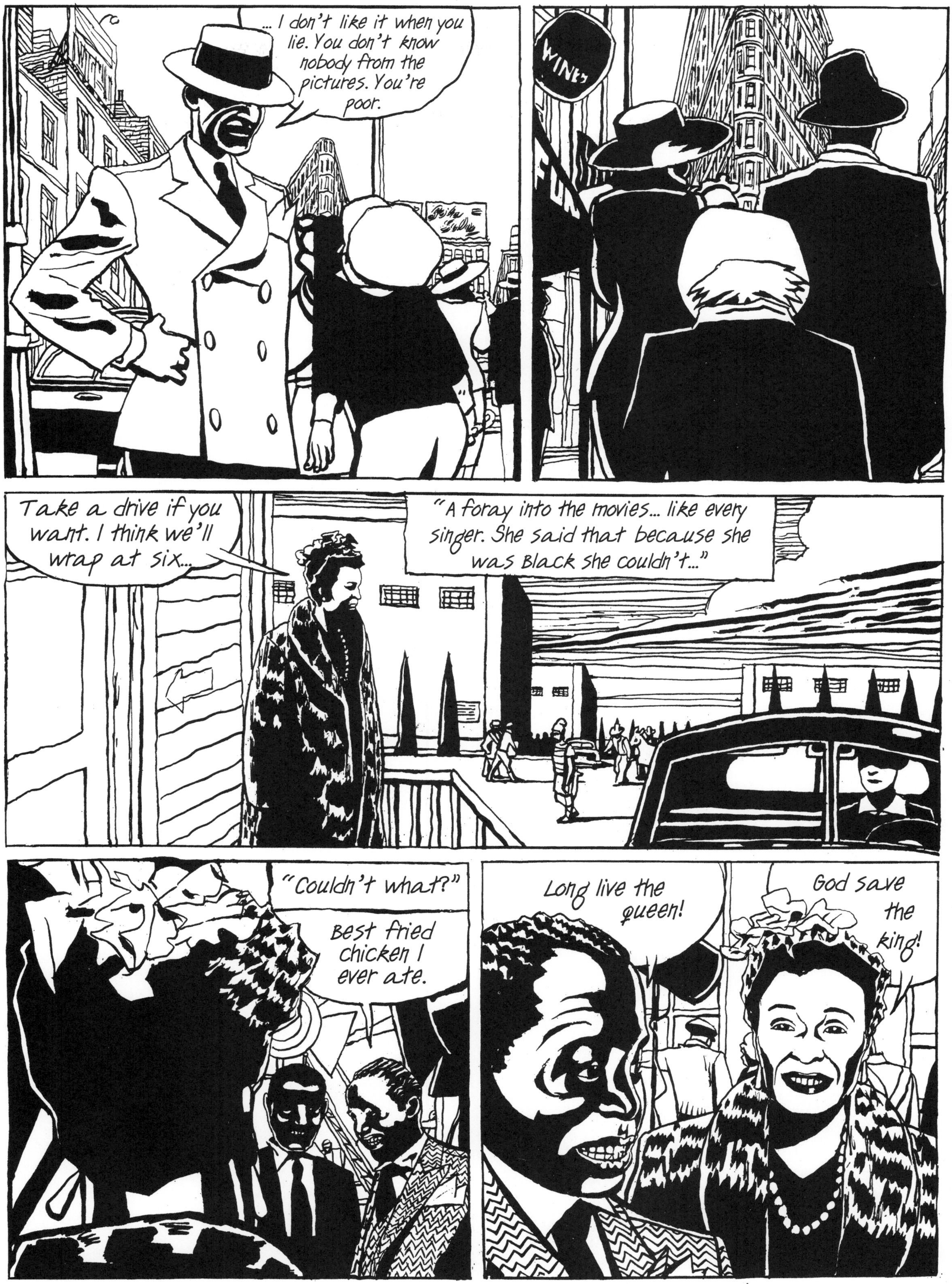

... I don't like it when you lie. You don't know nobody from the pictures. You're poor.
WINE
Take a drive if you want. I think we'll wrap at six...
"A foray into the movies... like every singer. She said that because she was Black she couldn't..."
"Couldn't what?"
Best fried chicken I ever ate.
Long live the queen!
God save the king!

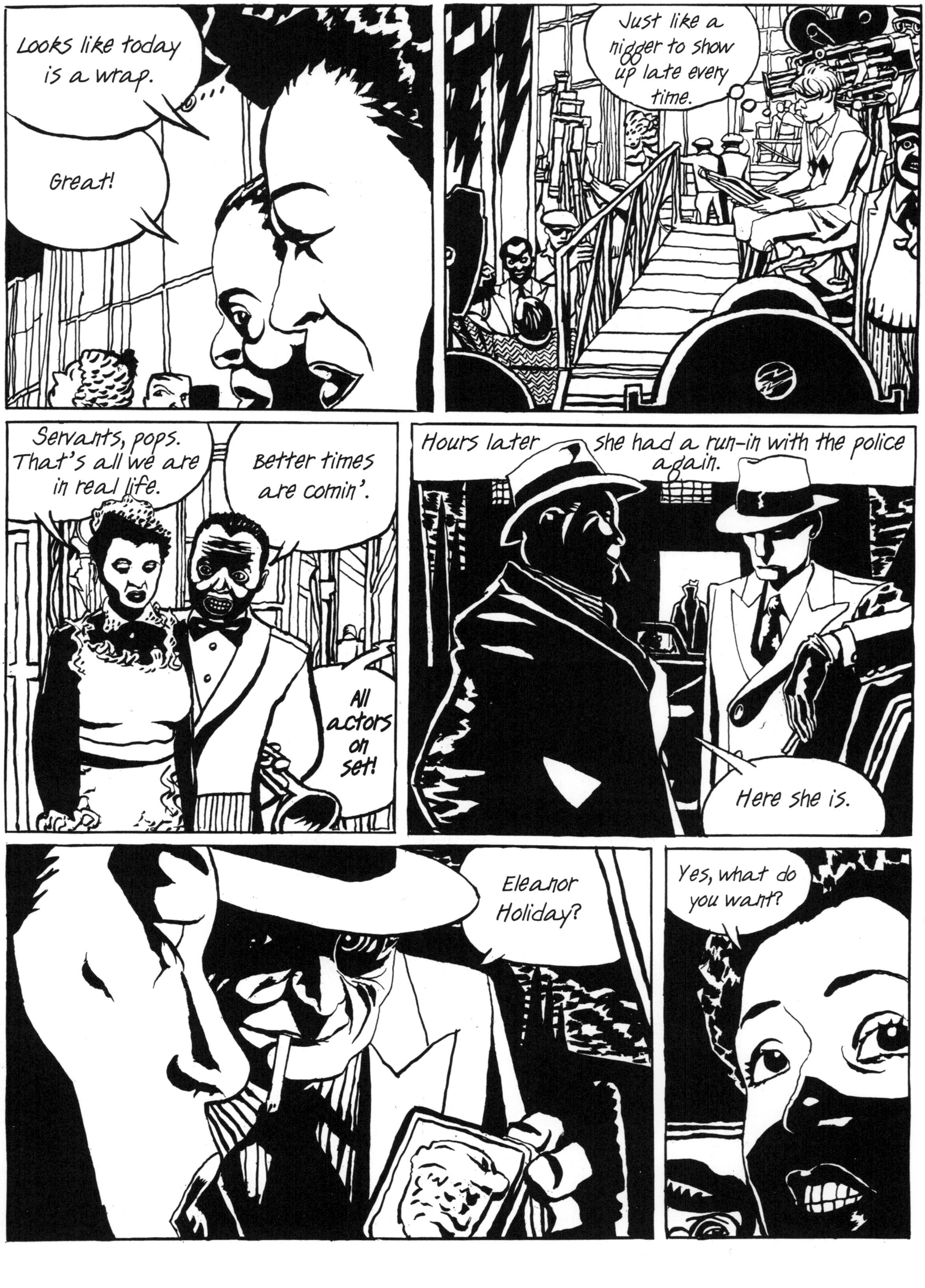
Looks like today is a wrap.
Great!
Just like a nigger to show up late every time.
Servants, pops. That's all we are in real life.
Better times are comin'.
All actors on set!
Hours later she had a run-in with the police again.
Here she is.
Eleanor Holiday?
Yes, what do you want?

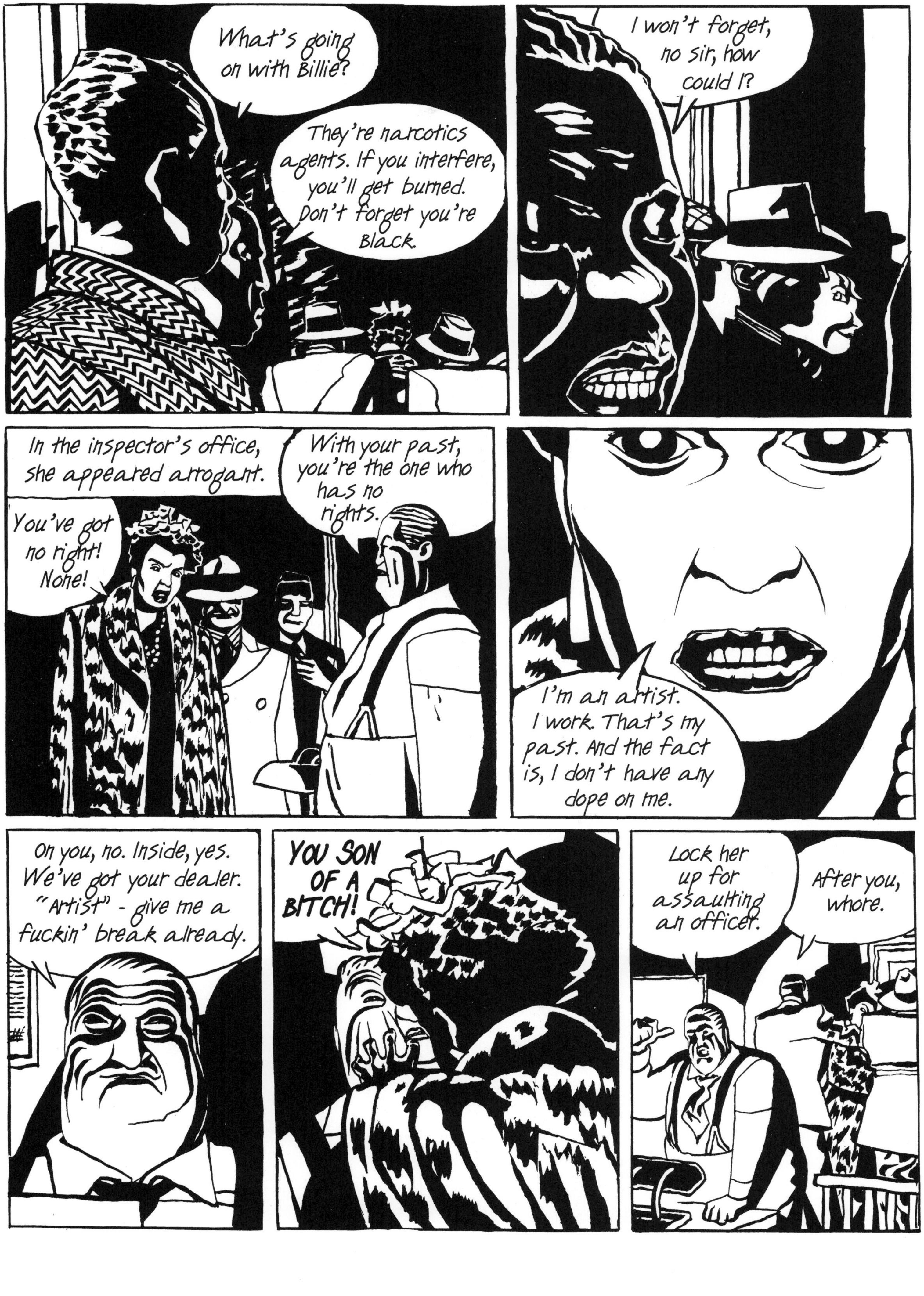
What's going on with Billie?
They're narcotics agents. If you interfere, you'll get burned. Don't forget you're Black.
I won't forget, no sir, how could I?
In the inspector's office, she appeared arrogant.
You've got no right! None!
With your past, you're the one who has no rights.
I'm an artist. I work. That's my past. And the fact is, I don't have any dope on me.
On you, no. Inside, yes. We've got your dealer. "Artist" - give me a fuckin' break already.
YOU SON OF A BITCH!
Lock her up for assaulting an officer.
After you, whore.

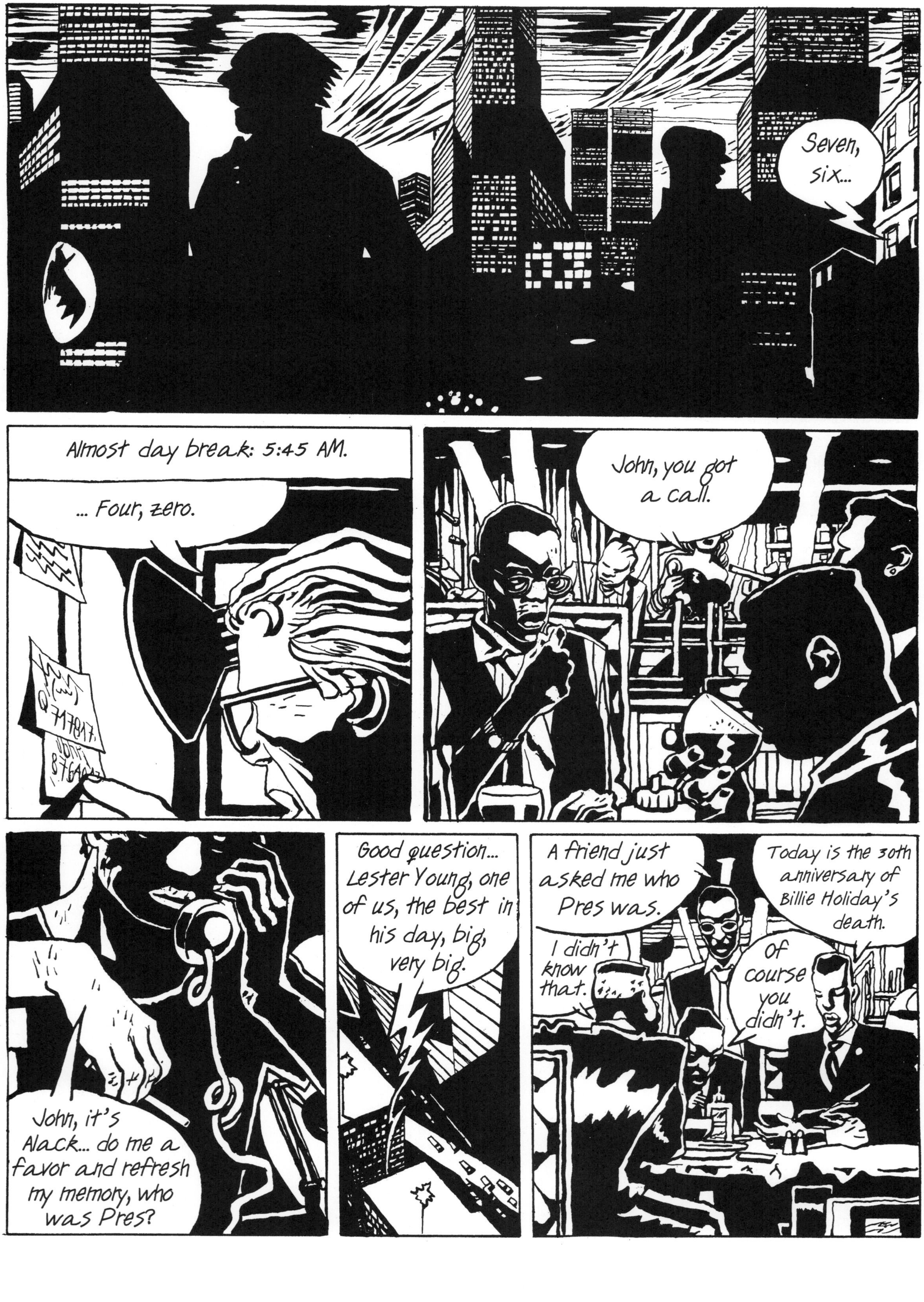
Seven, six...
Almost day break: 5:45 AM.
... Four, zero.
John, you got a call.
John, it's Alack... do me a favor and refresh my memory, who was Pres?
Good question... Lester Young, one of us, the best in his day, big, very big.
A friend just asked me who Pres was.
I didn't know that.
Today is the 30th anniversary of Billie Holiday's death.
Of course you didn't.

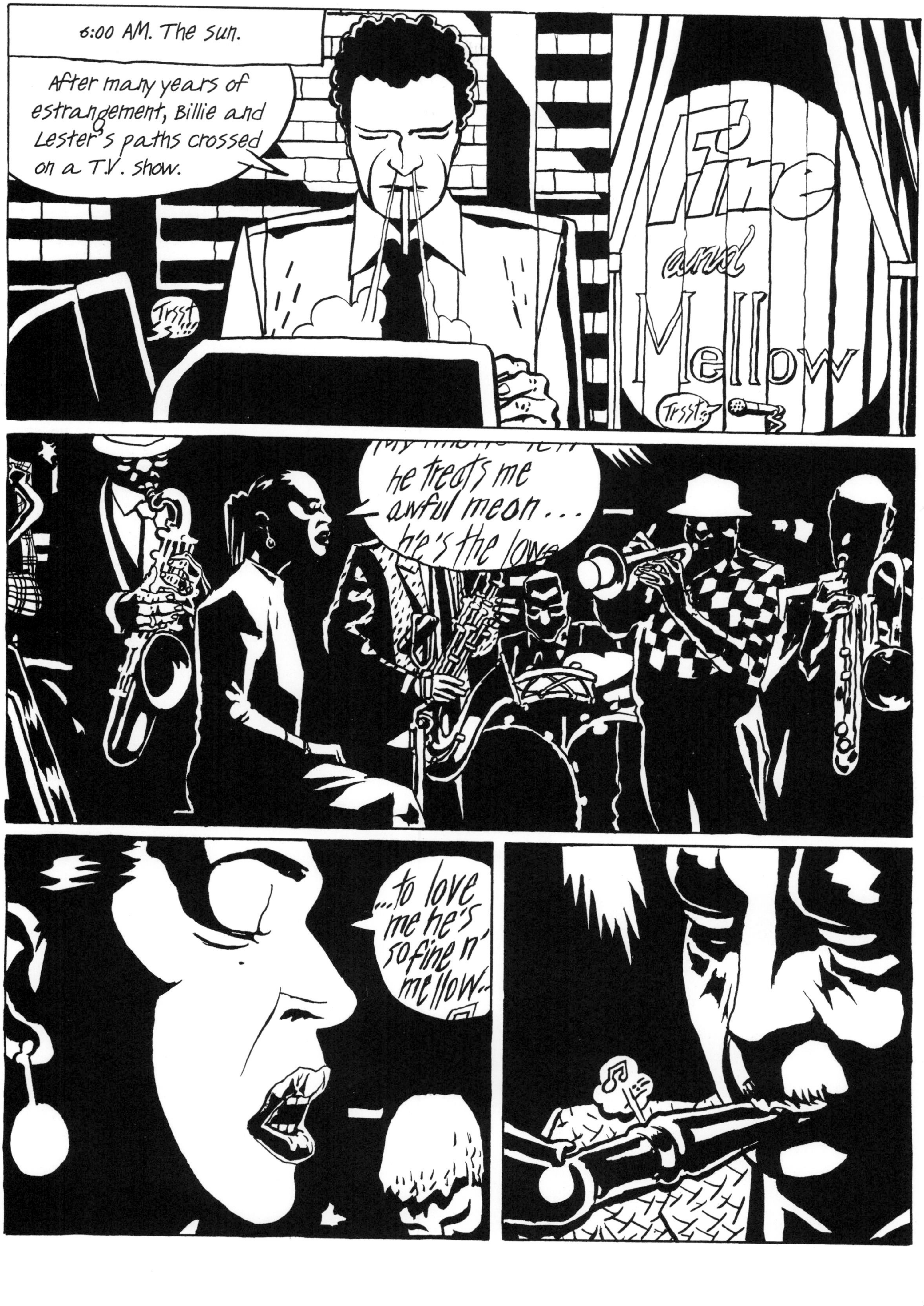
6:00 AM. The Sun.
After many years of estrangement, Billie and Lester's paths crossed on a T.V. show.
Trsst
Fine and Mellow
Trsst
he treats me awful mean...
...to love me he's so fine n' mellow...

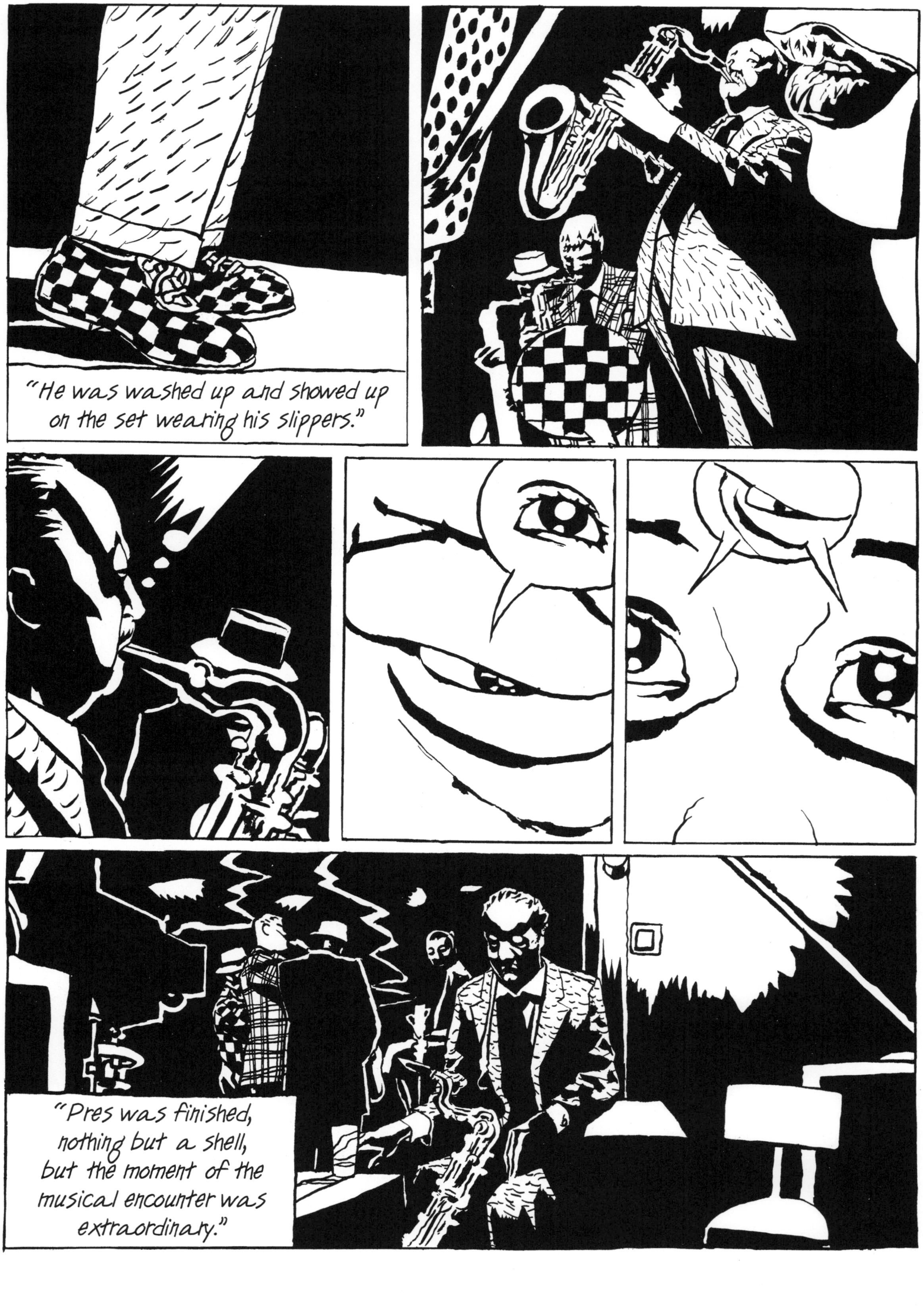
"He was washed up and showed up on the set wearing his slippers."
"Pres was finished, nothing but a shell, but the moment of the musical encounter was extraordinary."

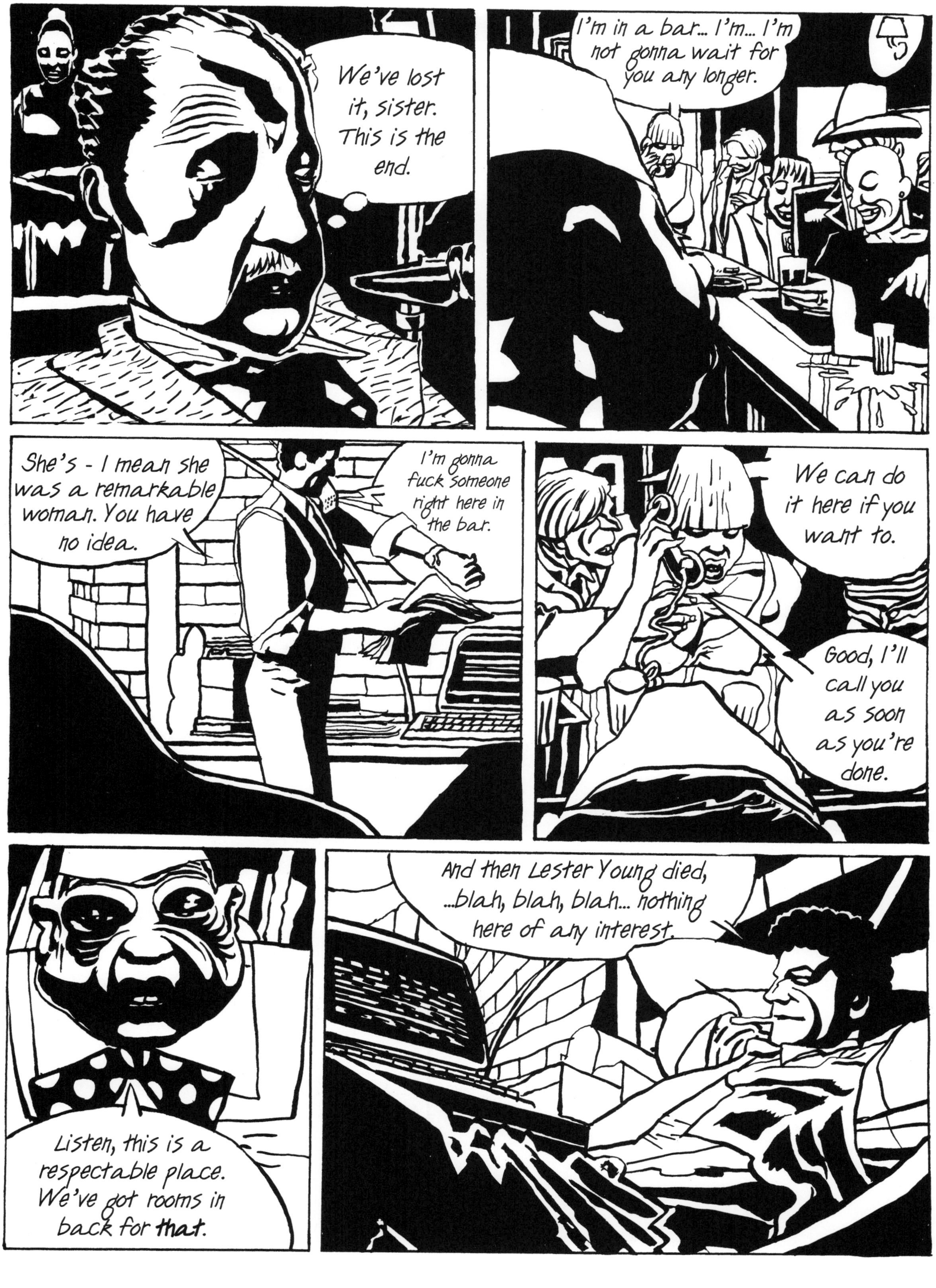
We've lost it, sister. This is the end.
I'm in a bar... I'm... I'm not gonna wait for you any longer.
She's - I mean she was a remarkable woman. You have no idea.
I'm gonna fuck someone right here in the bar.
We can do it here if you want to.
Good, I'll call you as soon as you're done.
Listen, this is a respectable place. We've got rooms in back for that.
And then Lester Young died, ...blah, blah, blah... nothing here of any interest.

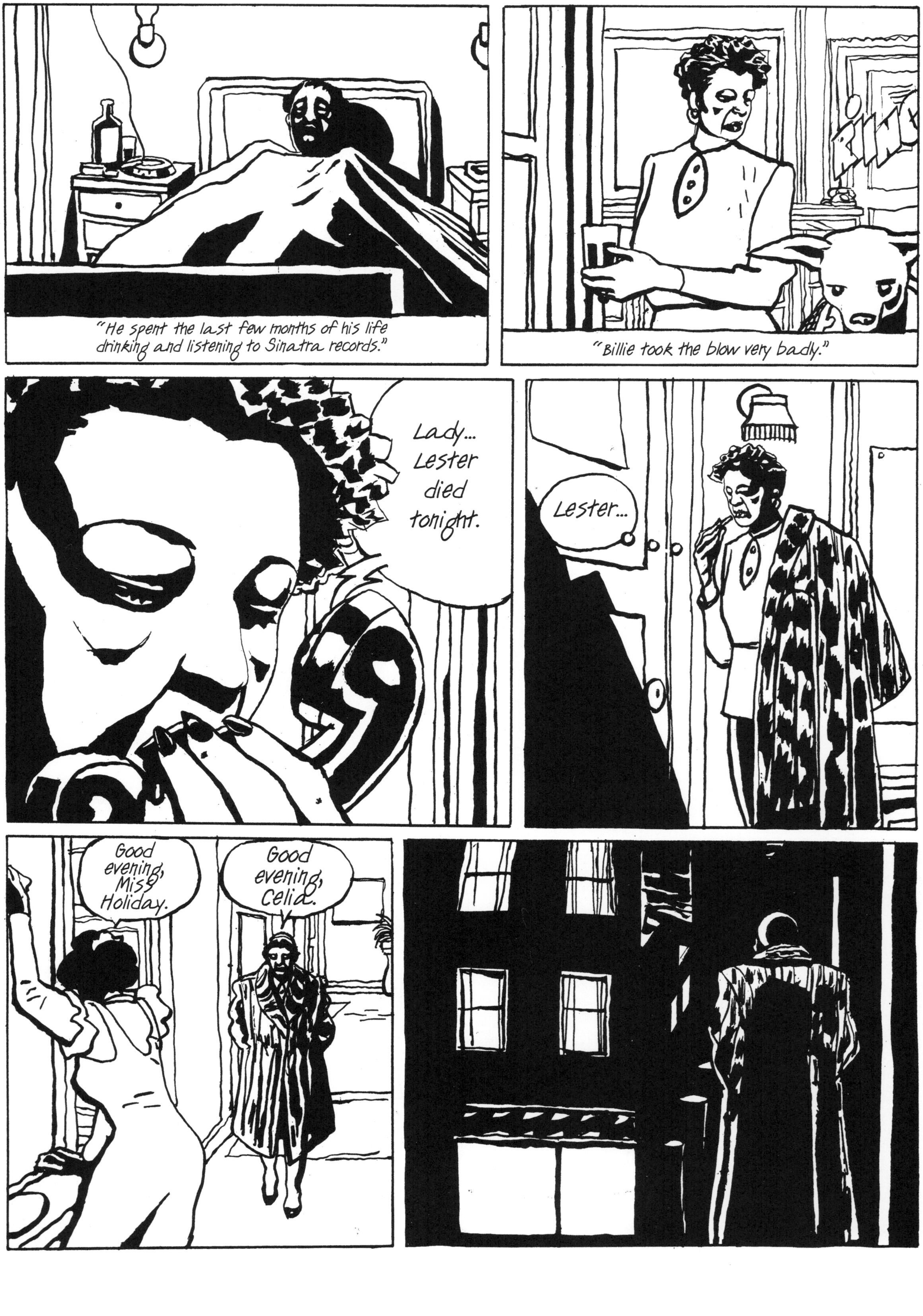
"He spent the last few months of his life drinking and listening to Sinatra records."
"Billie took the blow very badly."
Lady... Lester died tonight.
Lester...
Good evening, Miss Holiday.
Good evening, Celia.

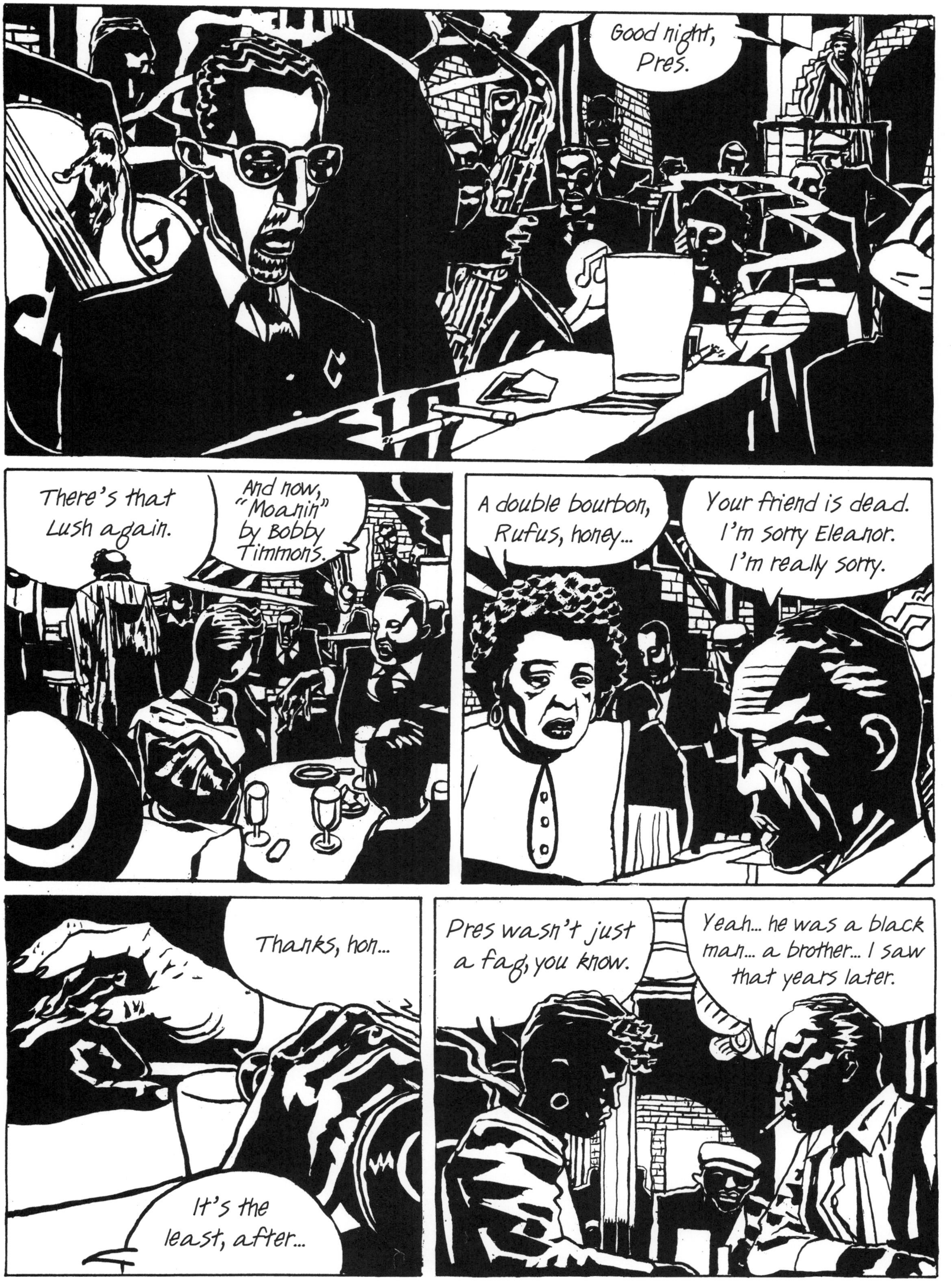
Good night, Pres.
There's that Lush again.
And now, "Moanin" by Bobby Timmons.
A double bourbon, Rufus, honey...
Your friend is dead. I'm sorry Eleanor. I'm really sorry.
Thanks, hon...
It's the least, after...
Pres wasn't just a fag, you know.
Yeah... he was a black man... a brother... I saw that years later.

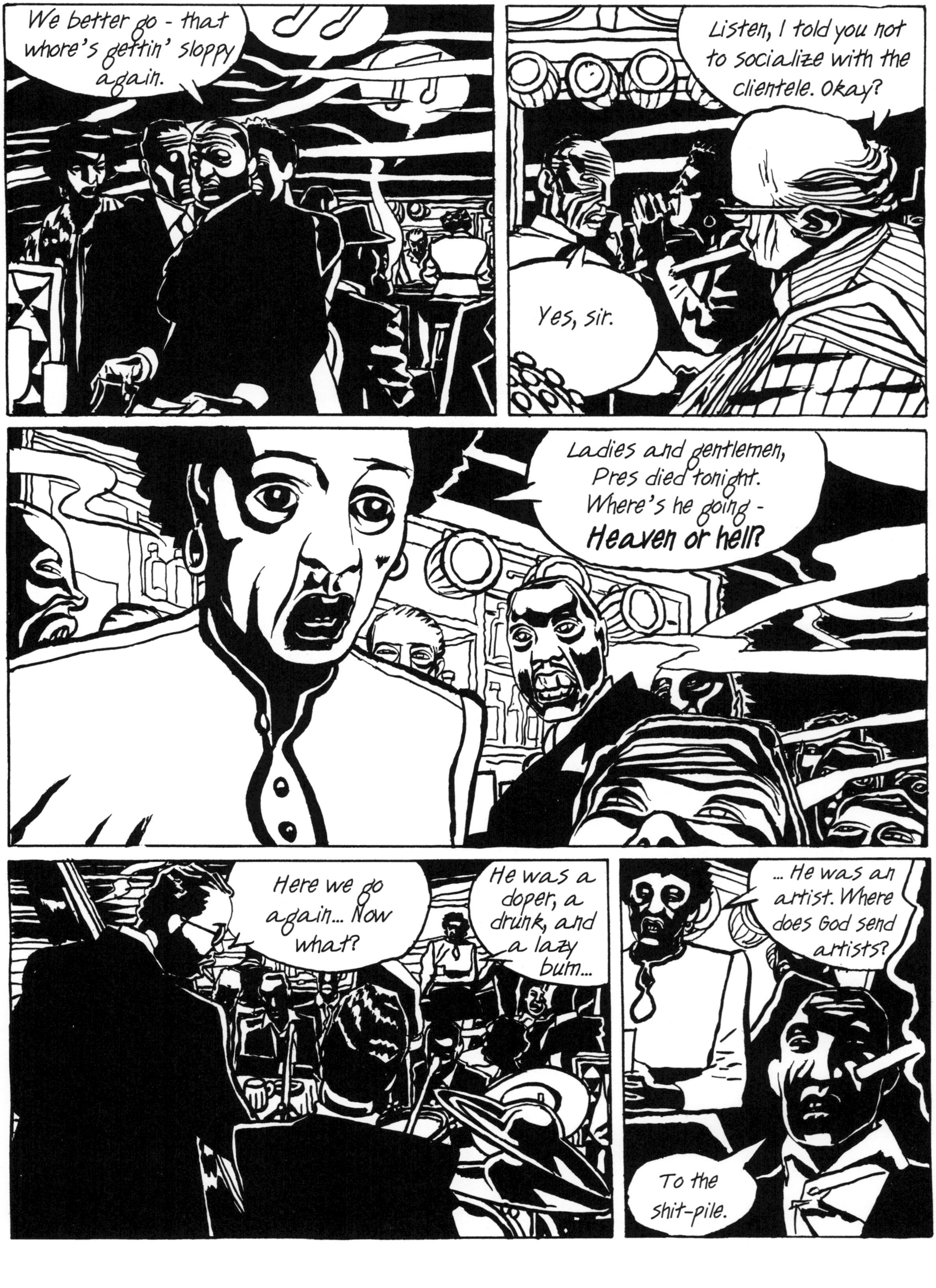
We better go - that whore's gettin' sloppy again.
Listen, I told you not to socialize with the clientele. Okay?
Yes, sir.
Ladies and gentlemen, Pres died tonight. Where's he going - Heaven or hell?
Here we go again... Now what?
He was a doper, a drunk, and a lazy bum...
... He was an artist. Where does God send artists?
To the shit-pile.

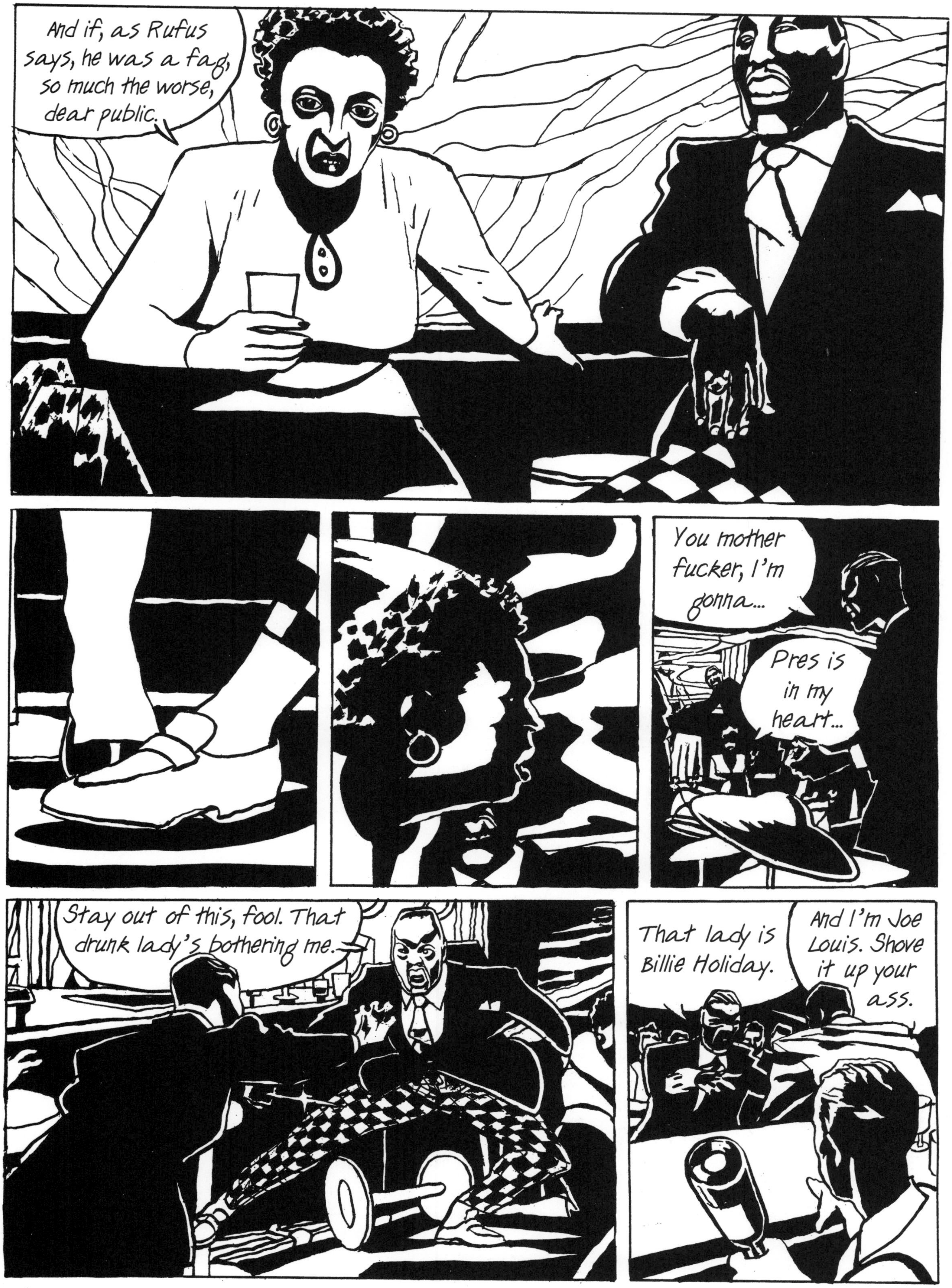

And if, as Rufus says, he was a fag, so much the worse, dear public.
You mother fucker, I'm gonna...
Pres is in my heart...
Stay out of this, fool. That drunk lady's bothering me.
That lady is Billie Holiday.
And I'm Joe Louis. Shove it up your ass.

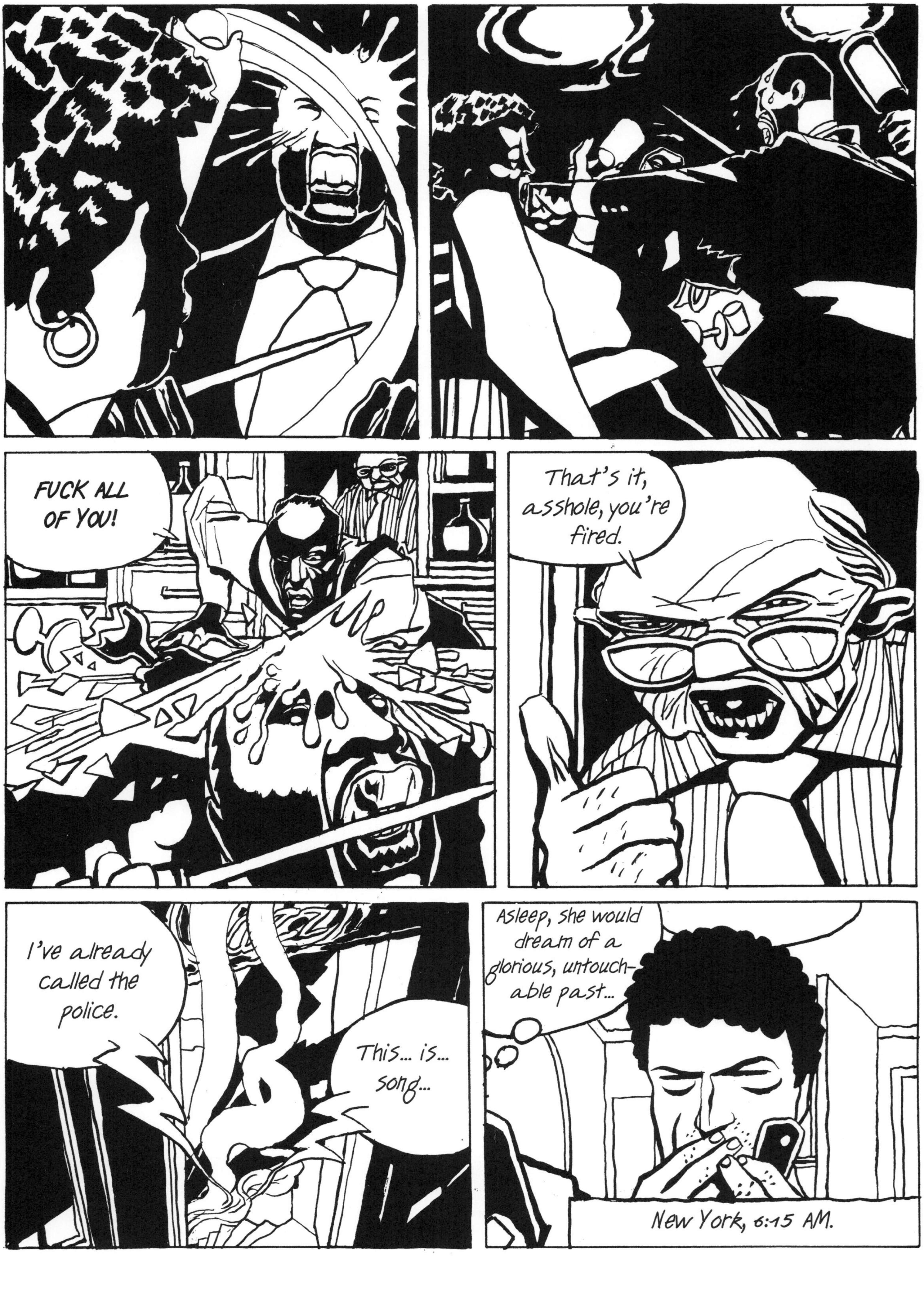
FUCK ALL OF YOU!
That's it, asshole, you're fired.
I've already called the police.
This... is... song...
Asleep, she would dream of a glorious, untouchable past...
New York, 6:15 AM.

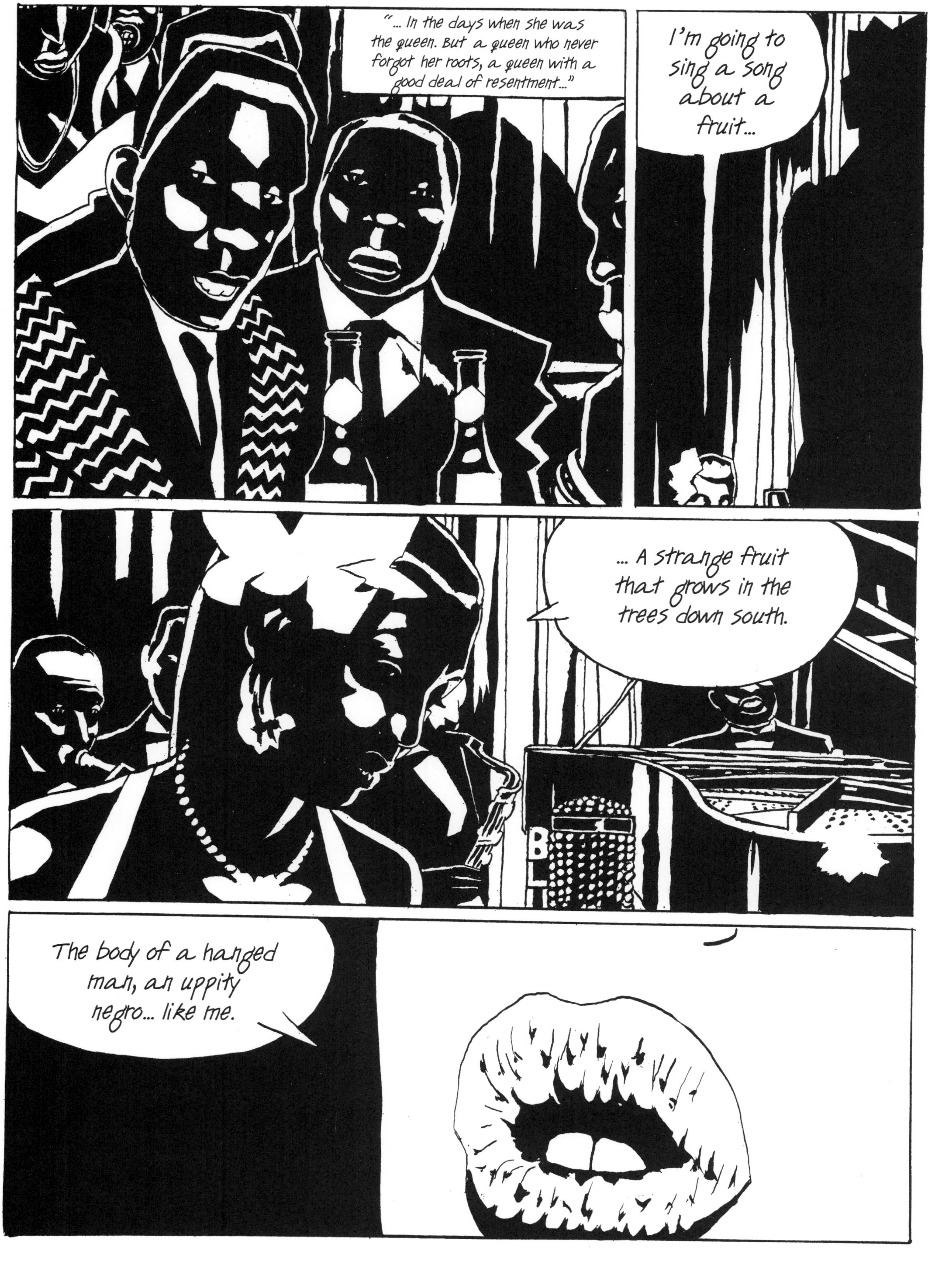
"... In the days when she was the queen. But a queen who never forgot her roots, a queen with a good deal of resentment..."
I'm going to sing a song about a fruit...
... A strange fruit that grows in the trees down south.
BL
The body of a hanged man, an uppity negro... like me.

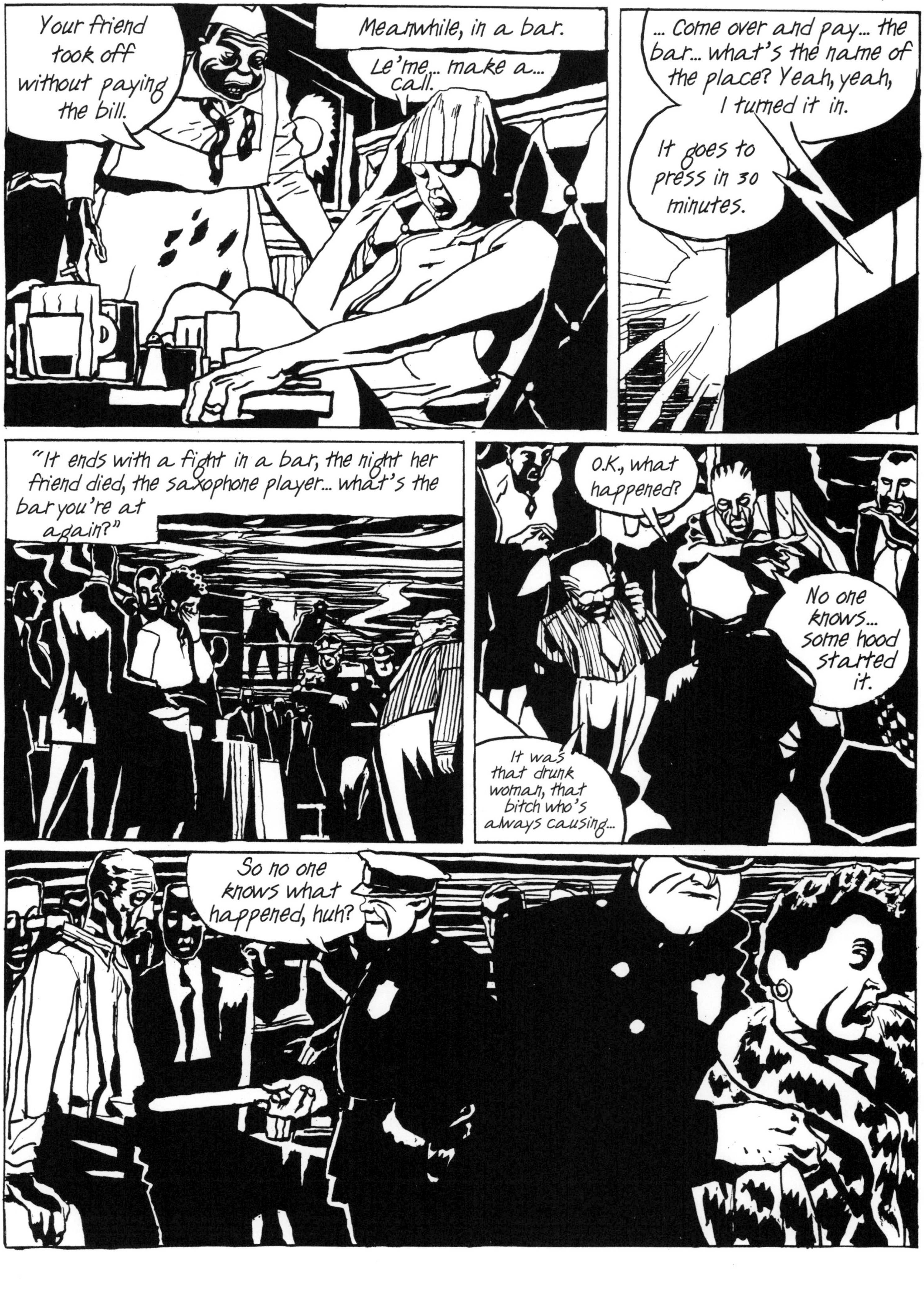
Your friend took off without paying the bill.
Meanwhile, in a bar.
Le'me... make a... call.
... Come over and pay... the bar... what's the name of the place? Yeah, yeah, I turned it in.
It goes to press in 30 minutes.
"It ends with a fight in a bar, the night her friend died, the saxophone player... what's the bar you're at again?"
O.K., what happened?
No one knows... some hood started it.
It was that drunk woman, that bitch who's always causing...
So no one knows what happened, huh?

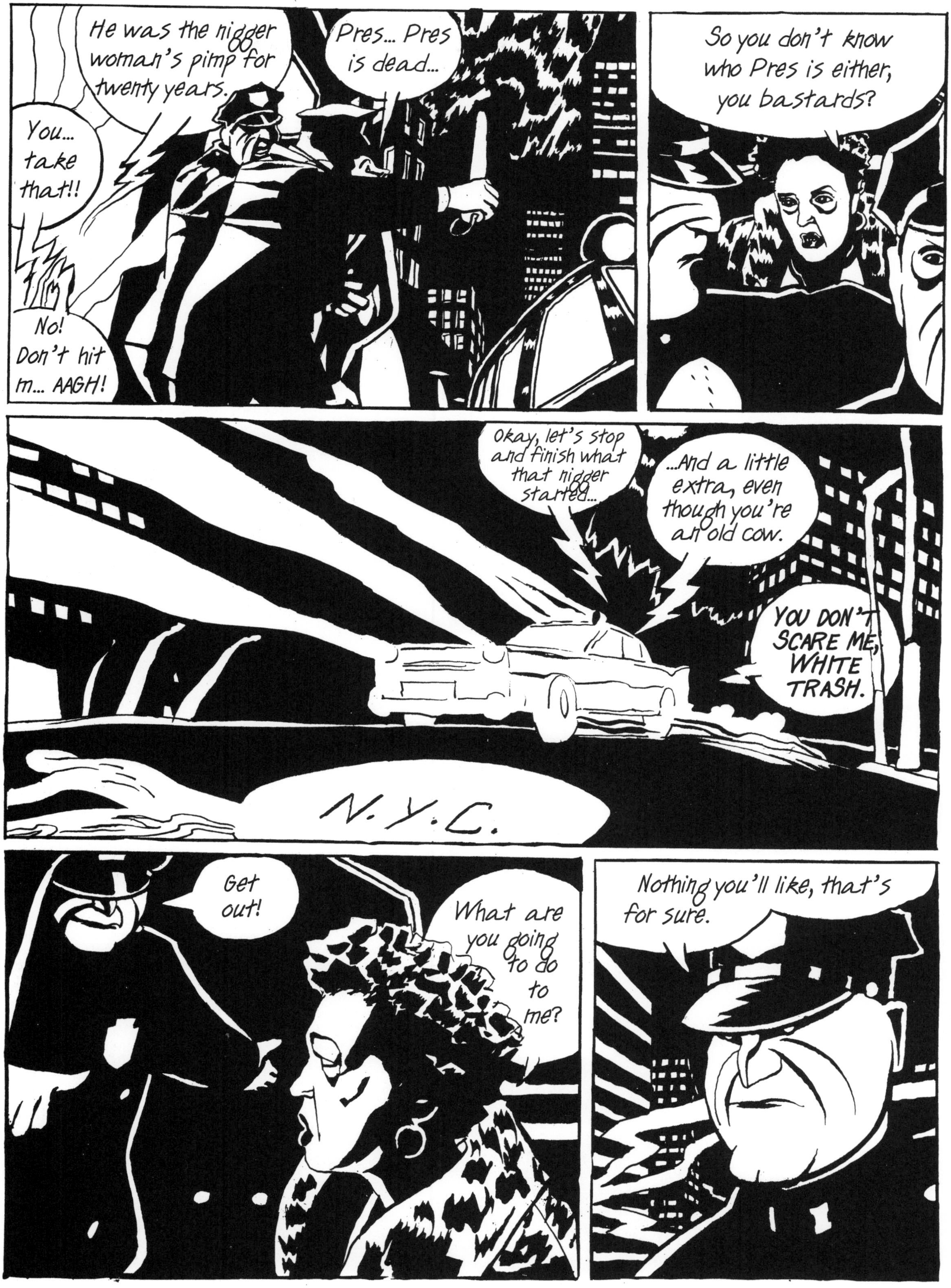
He was the nigger woman's pimp for twenty years.
Pres... Pres is dead...
You... take that!!
No! Don't hit m... AAGH!
So you don't know who Pres is either, you bastards?
Okay, let's stop and finish what that nigger started...
...And a little extra, even though you're an old cow.
YOU DON'T SCARE ME, WHITE TRASH.
N.Y.C.
Get out!
What are you going to do to me?
Nothing you'll like, that's for sure.

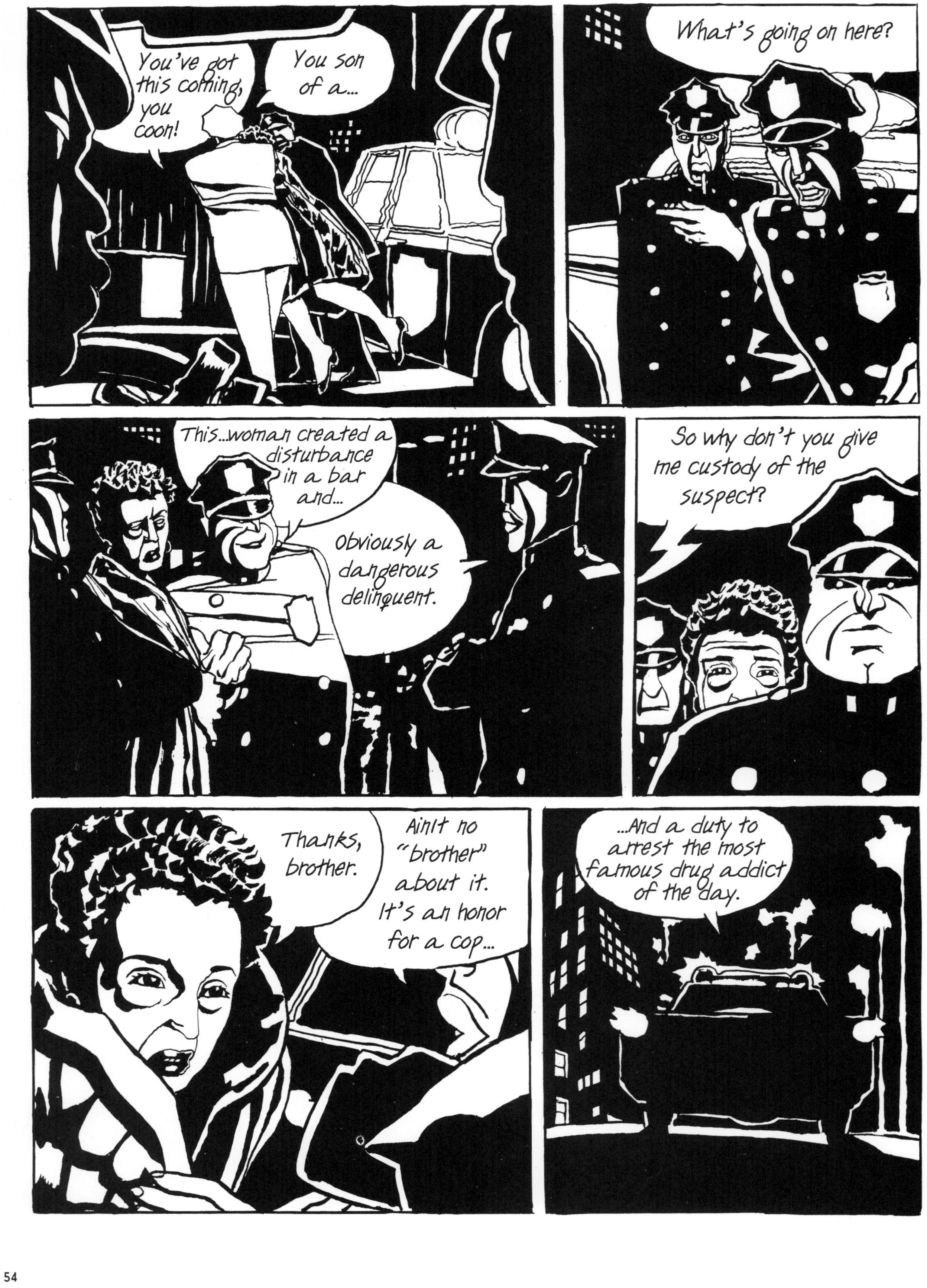
You've got this coming, you coon!
You son of a...
What's going on here?
This...woman created a disturbance in a bar and...
Obviously a dangerous delinquent.
So why don't you give me custody of the suspect?
Thanks, brother.
Ain't no "brother" about it. It's an honor for a cop...
...And a duty to arrest the most famous drug addict of the day.

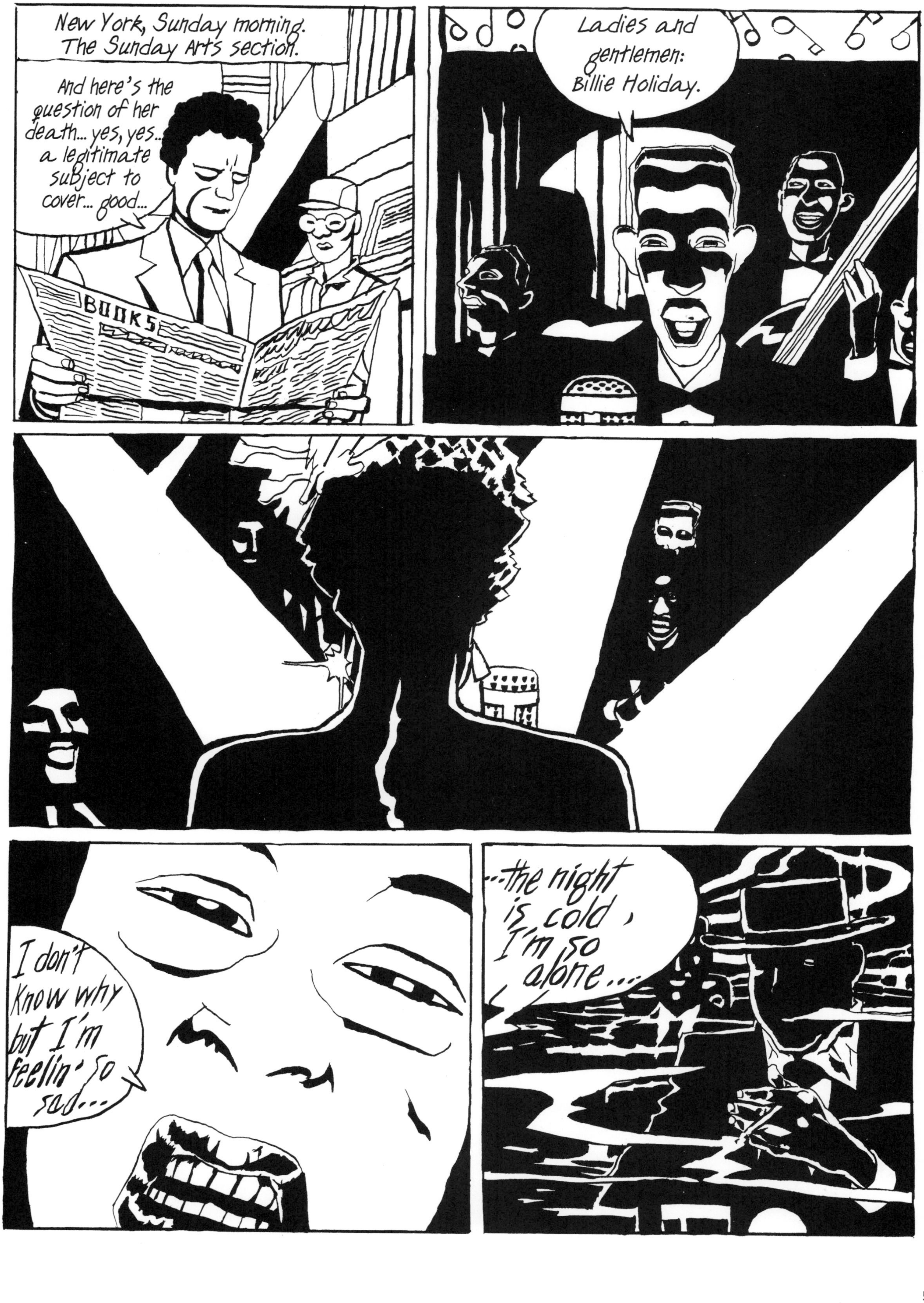

New York, Sunday morning.
The Sunday Arts section.
And here's the question of her death... yes, yes... a legitimate subject to cover... good...
BOOKS
Ladies and gentlemen: Billie Holiday.
I don't know why but I'm feelin' so sad...
...the night is cold, I'm so alone...

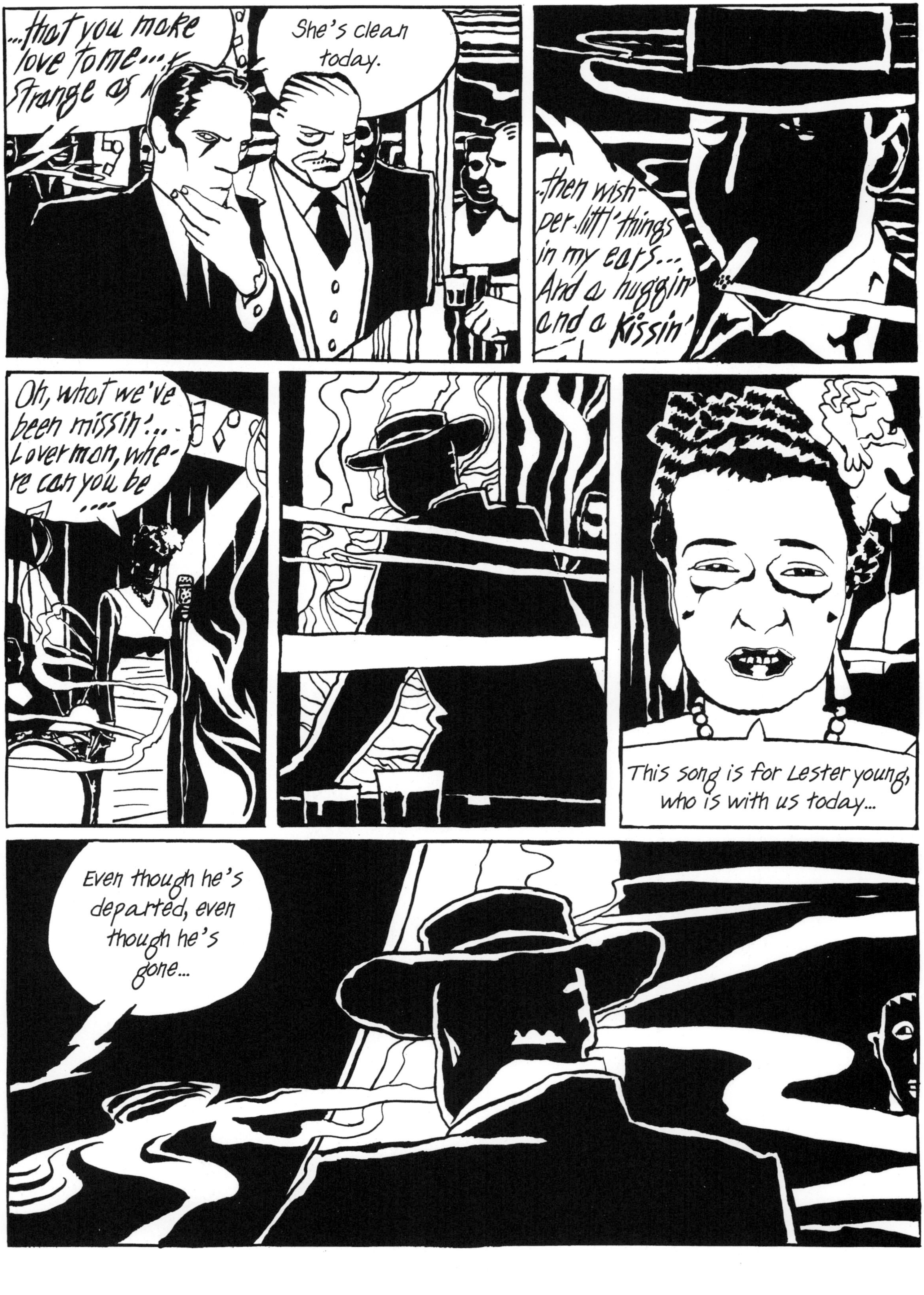

...that you make love to me...
Strange as
She's clean today.
...then wish-per littl' things in my ears... And a huggin' and a kissin'
Oh, what we've been missin'... Lover man, whe-re can you be ....
This song is for Lester young, who is with us today...
Even though he's departed, even though he's gone...

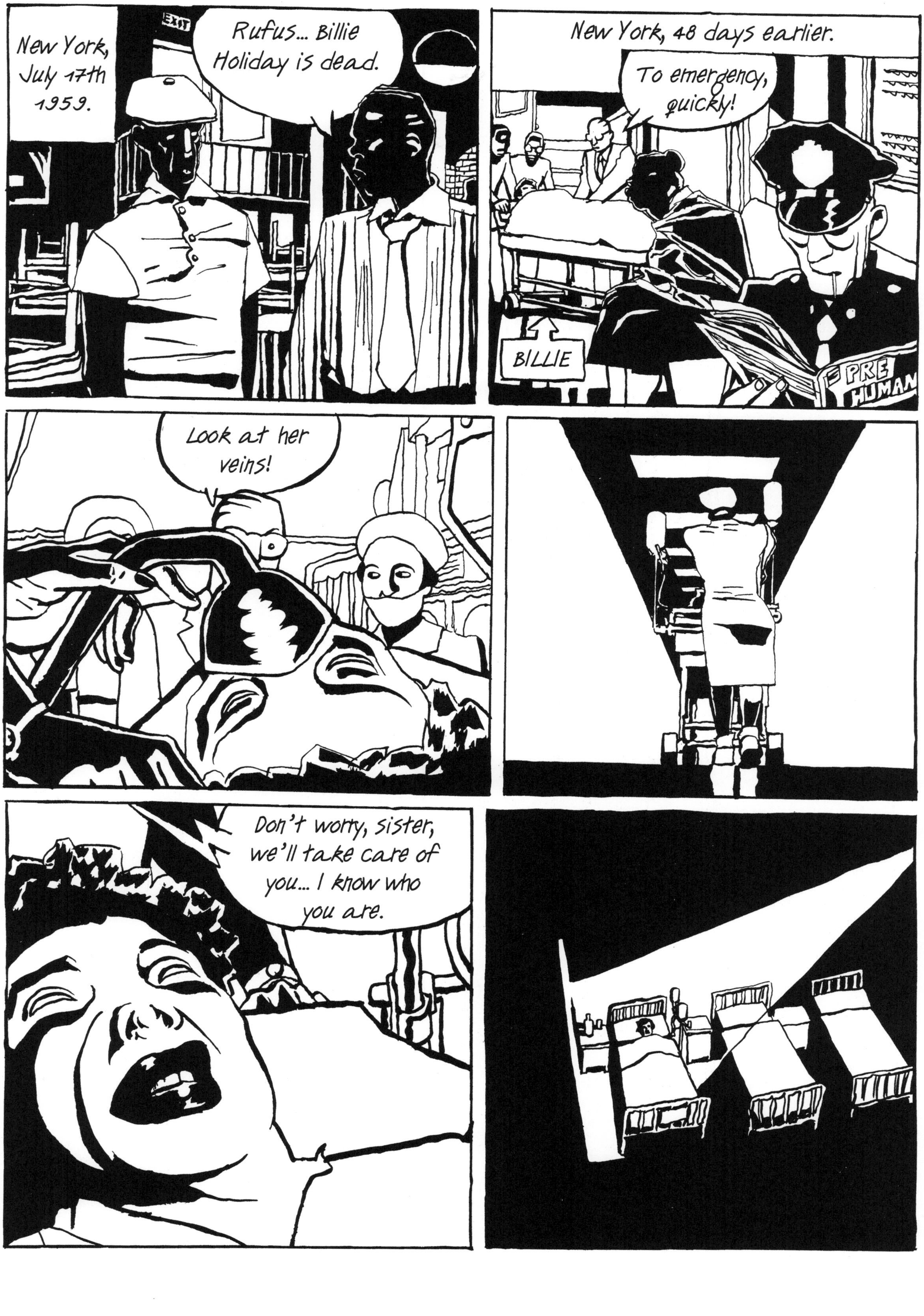
New York, July 17th 1959.
EXIT
Rufus... Billie Holiday is dead.
New York, 48 days earlier.
To emergency, quickly!
BILLIE
PRE HUMAN
Look at her veins!
Don't worry, sister, we'll take care of you... I know who you are.

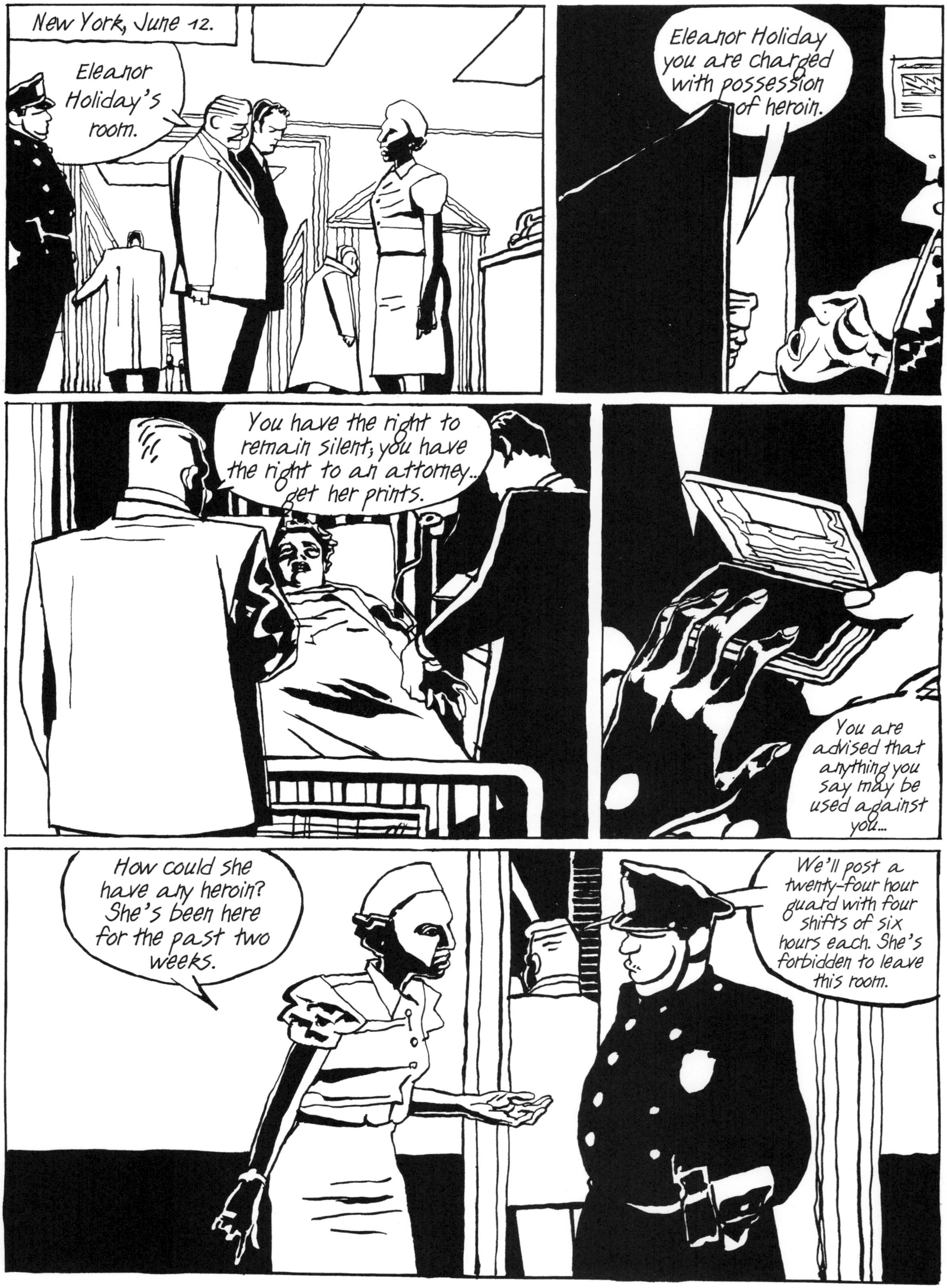

New York, June 12.
Eleanor Holiday's room.
Eleanor Holiday you are charged with possession of heroin.
You have the right to remain silent; you have the right to an attorney... get her prints.
You are advised that anything you say may be used against you...
How could she have any heroin? She's been here for the past two weeks.
We'll post a twenty-four hour guard with four shifts of six hours each. She's forbidden to leave this room.

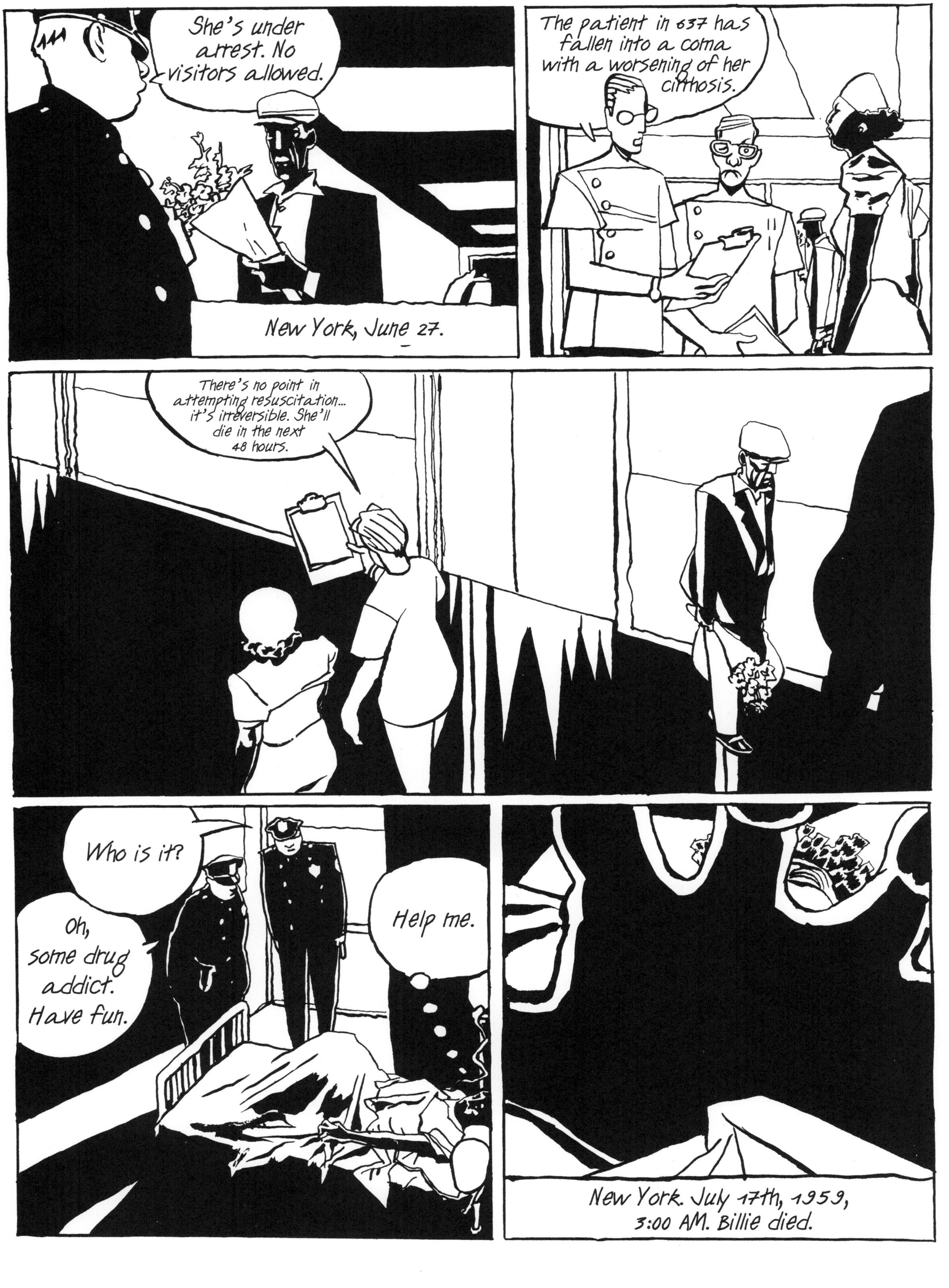

She's under arrest. No visitors allowed.
New York, June 27.
The patient in 637 has fallen into a coma with a worsening of her cirrhosis.
There's no point in attempting resuscitation... it's irreversible. She'll die in the next 48 hours.
Who is it?
Oh, some drug addict. Have fun.
Help me.
New York. July 17th, 1959, 3:00 AM. Billie died.

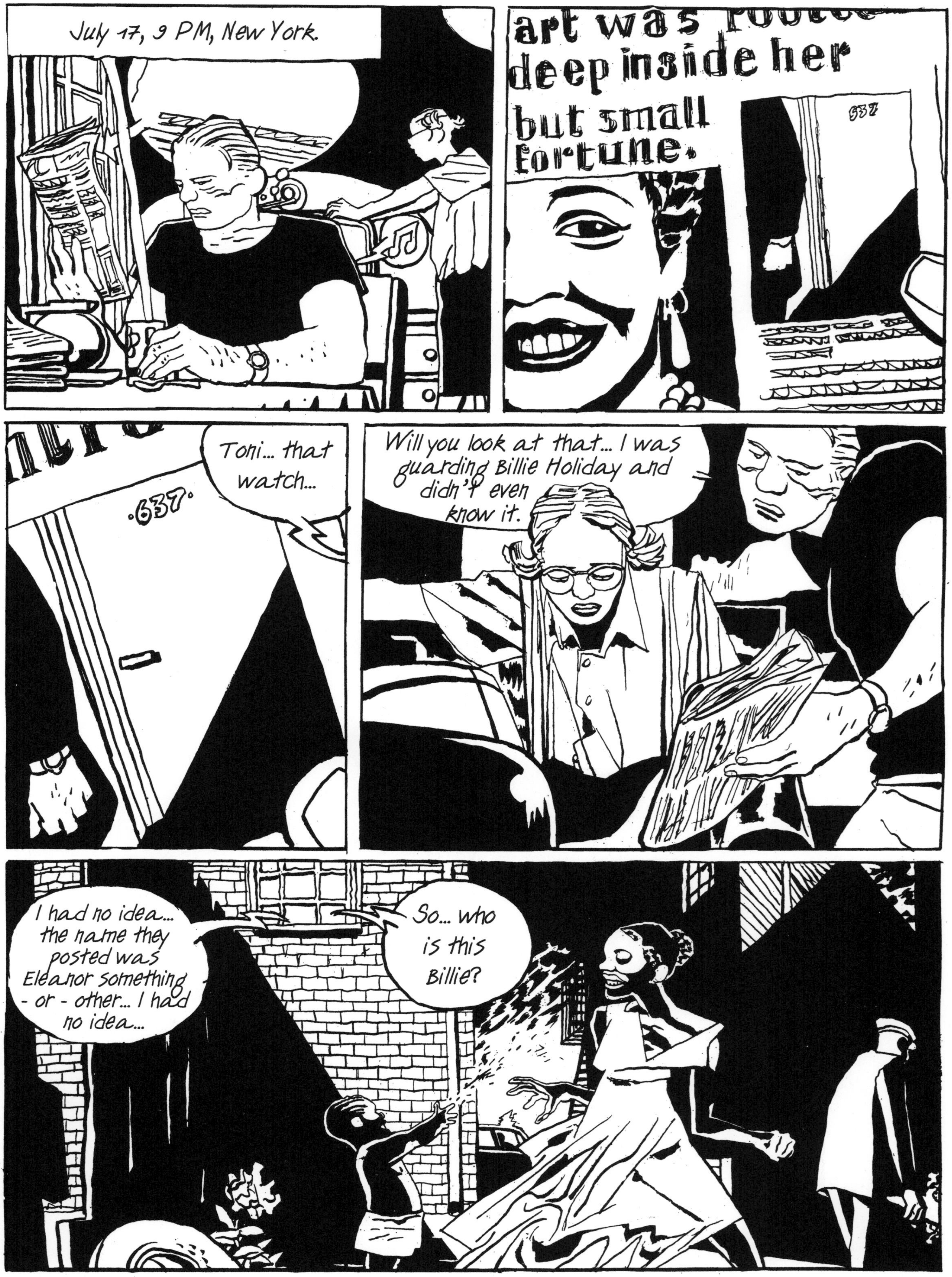
July 17, 9 PM, New York.
art was
deep inside her
but small
fortune.
·637·
Toni... that watch...
Will you look at that... I was guarding Billie Holiday and didn't even know it.
I had no idea... the name they posted was Eleanor something - or - other... I had no idea...
So... who is this Billie?

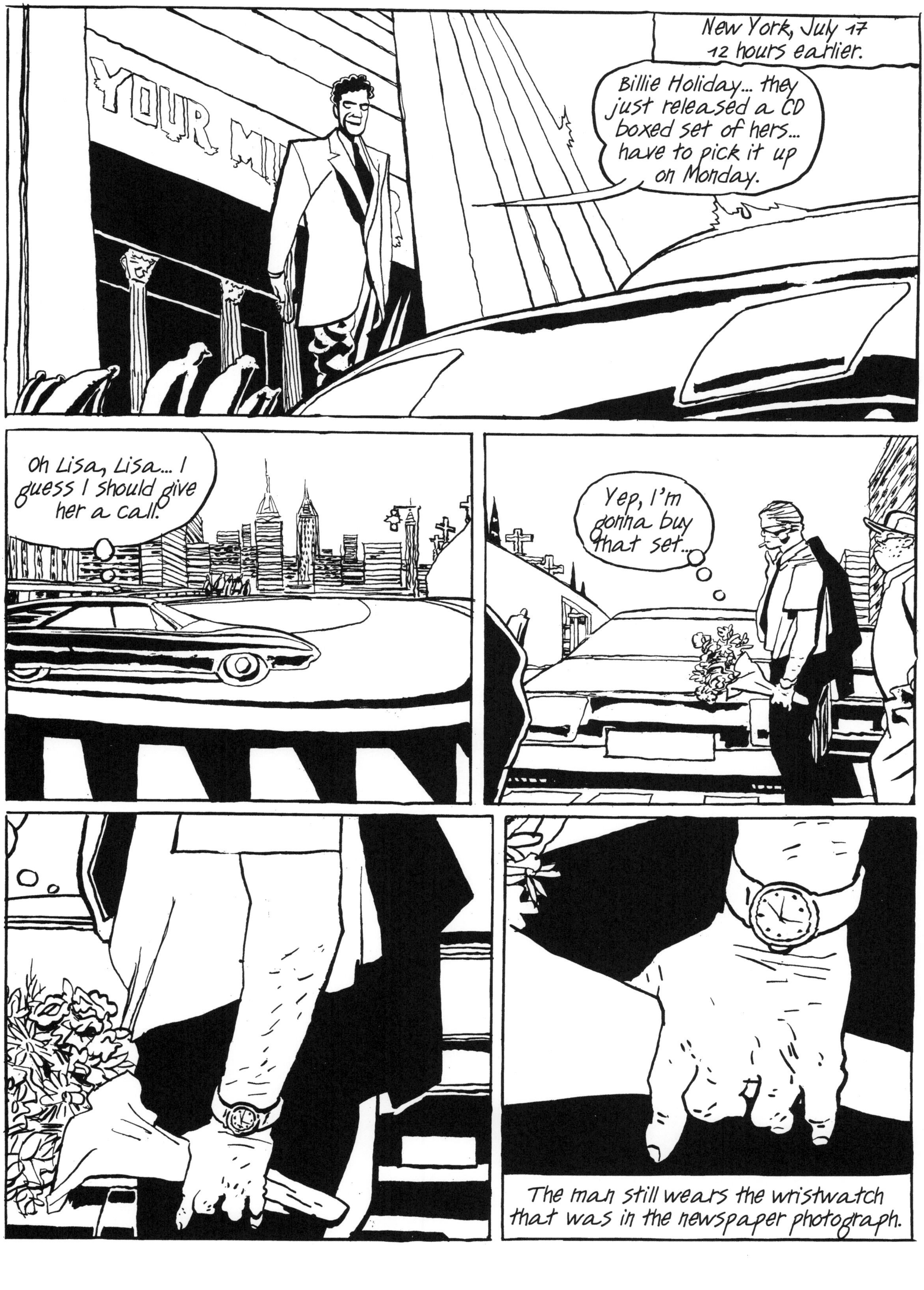
New York, July 17
12 hours earlier.
Billie Holiday... they just released a CD boxed set of hers... have to pick it up on Monday.
YOUR
Oh Lisa, Lisa... I guess I should give her a call.
Yep, I'm gonna buy that set...
The man still wears the wristwatch that was in the newspaper photograph.

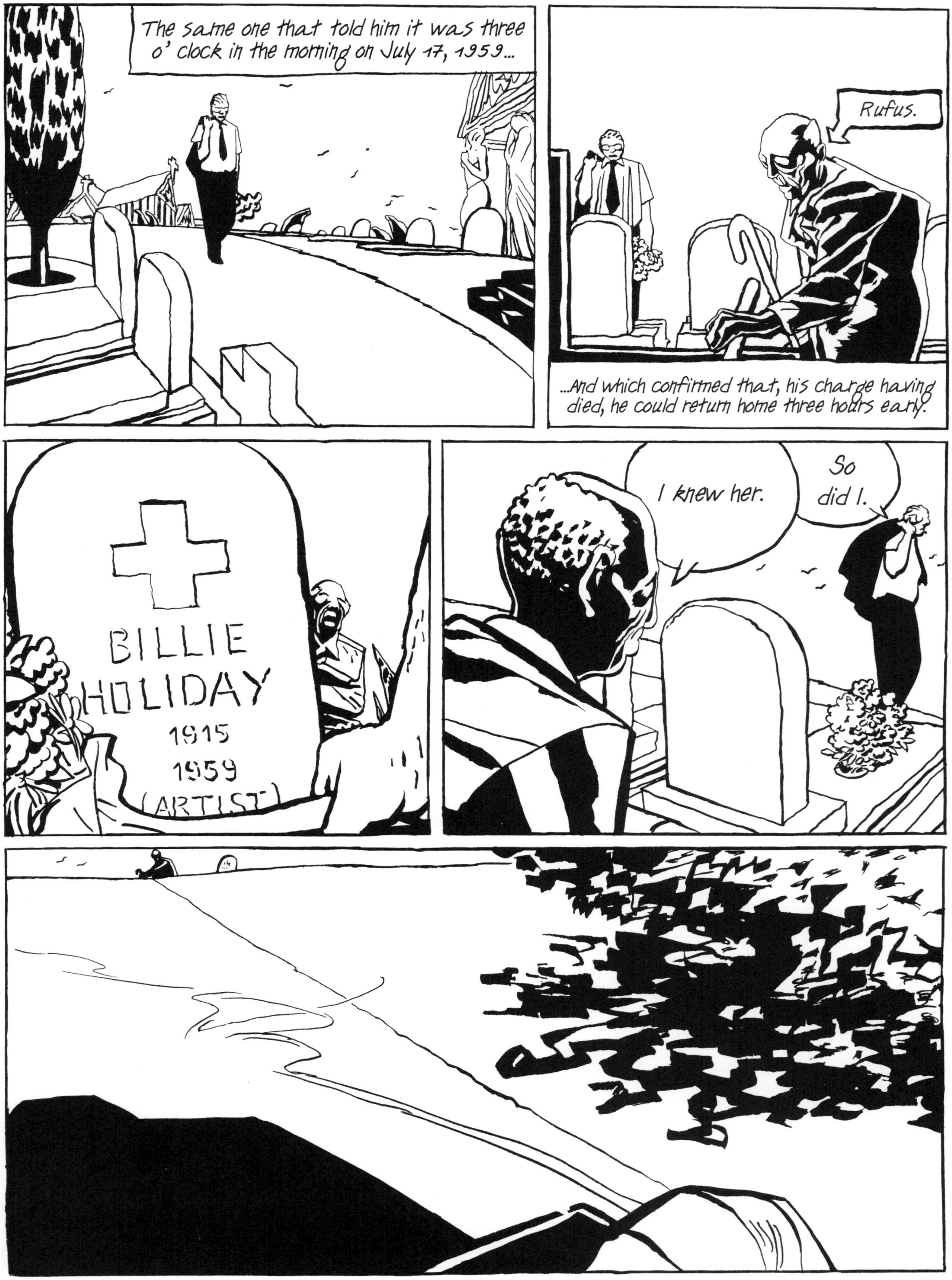

The same one that told him it was three o' clock in the morning on July 17, 1959...
Rufus.
...And which confirmed that, his charge having died, he could return home three hours early.
BILLIE HOLIDAY 1915 1959 (ARTIST)
I knew her.
So did I.

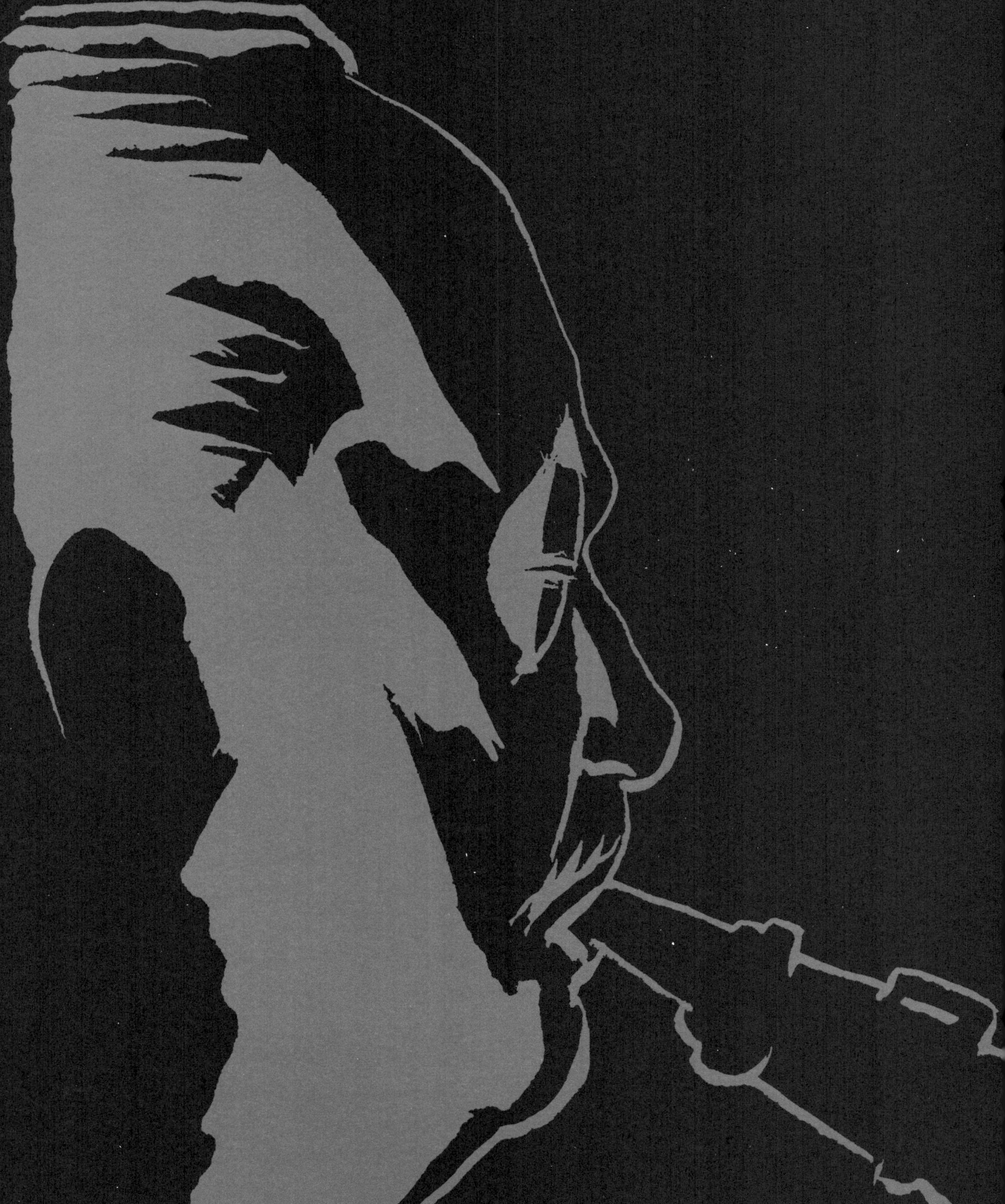

JAZZSESSIONS

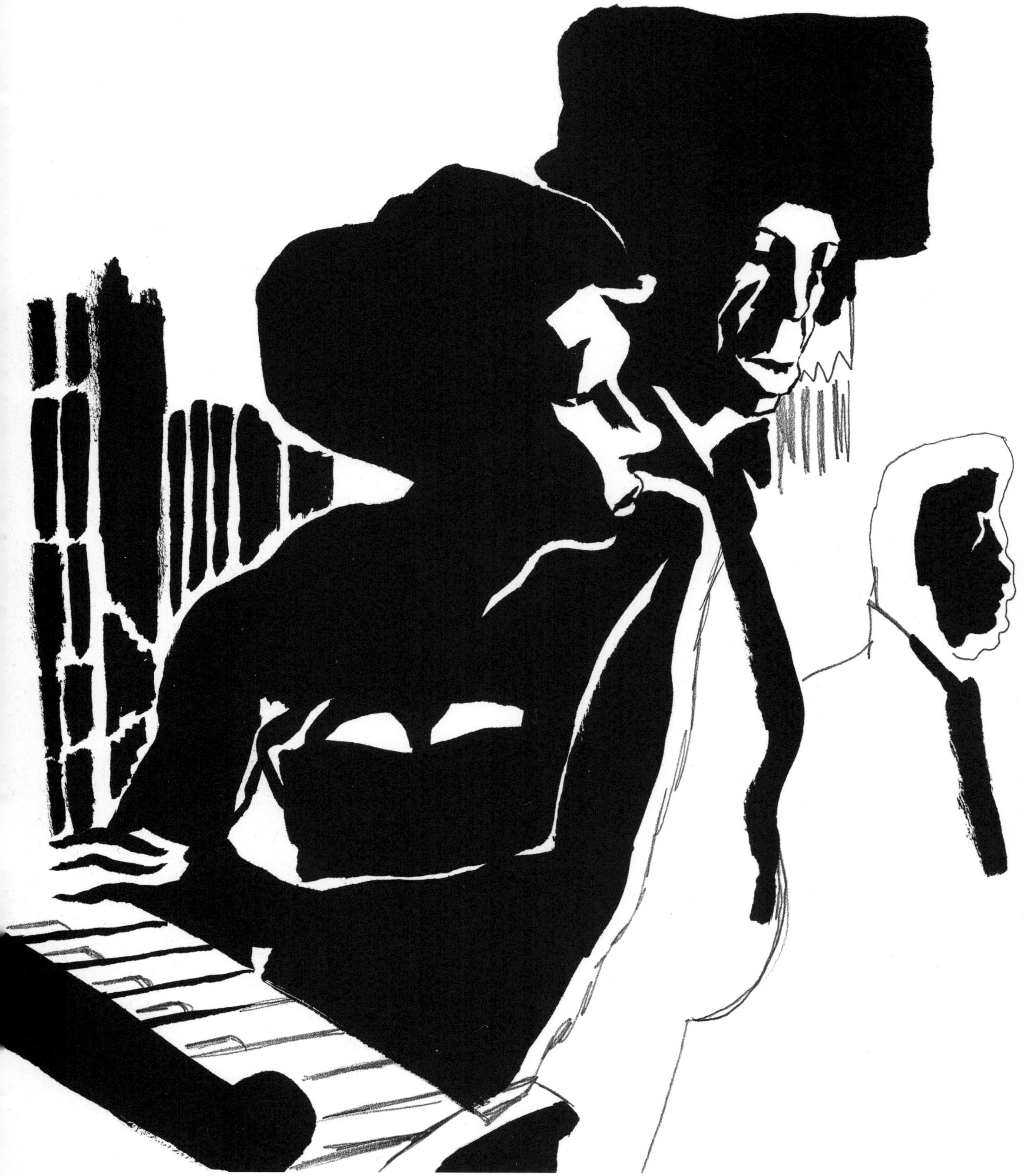

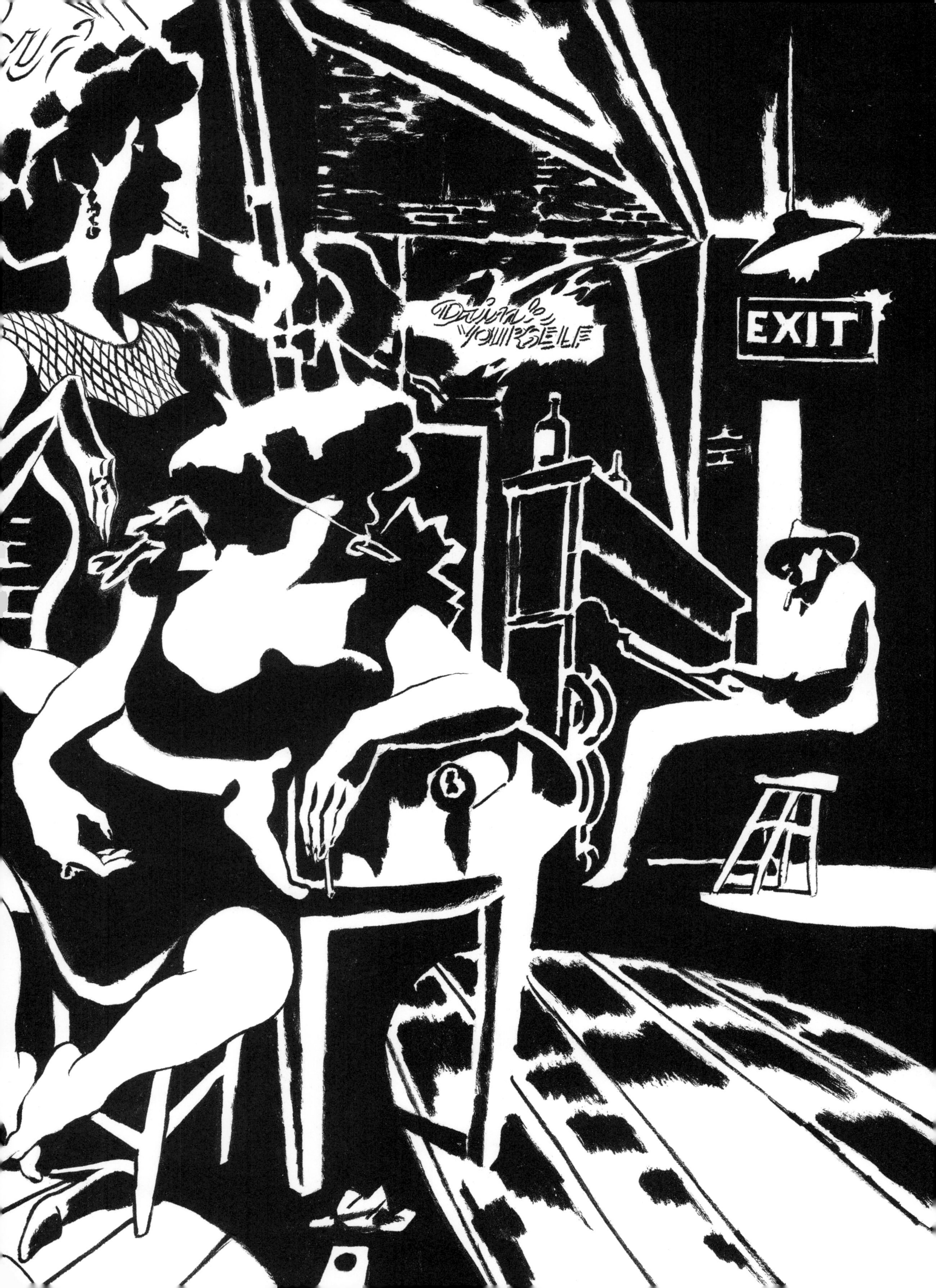
YOURSELF
EXIT

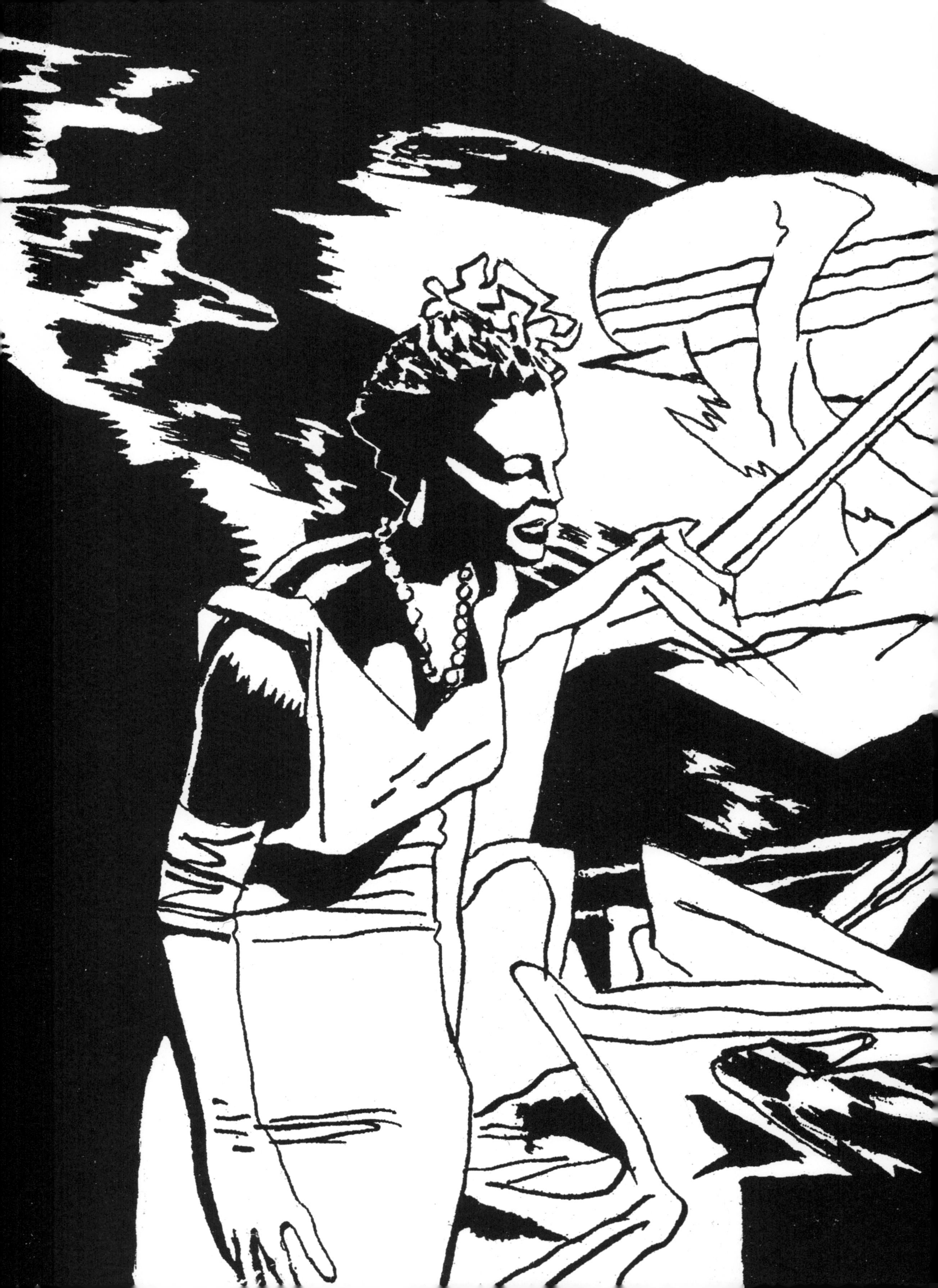

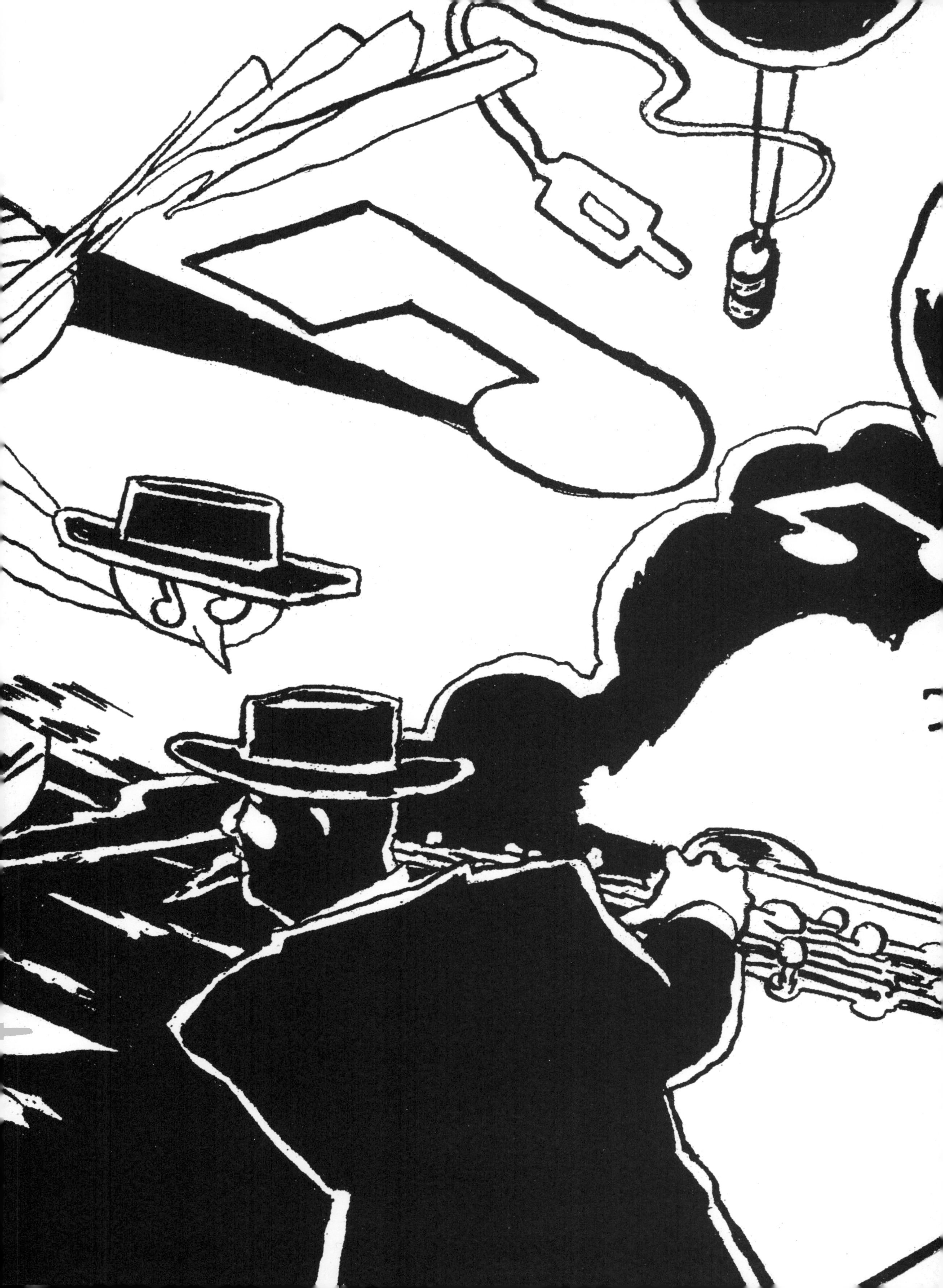

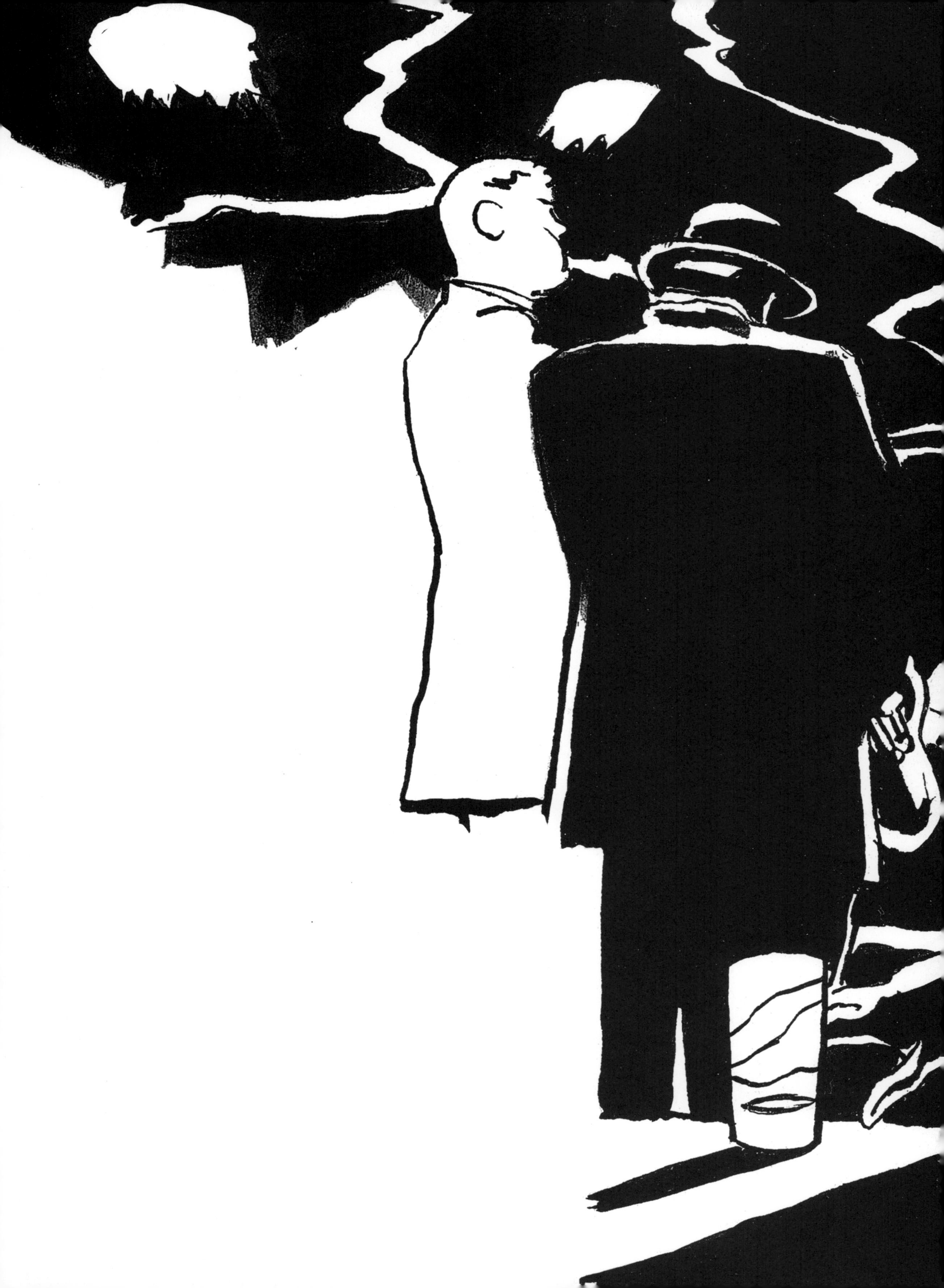

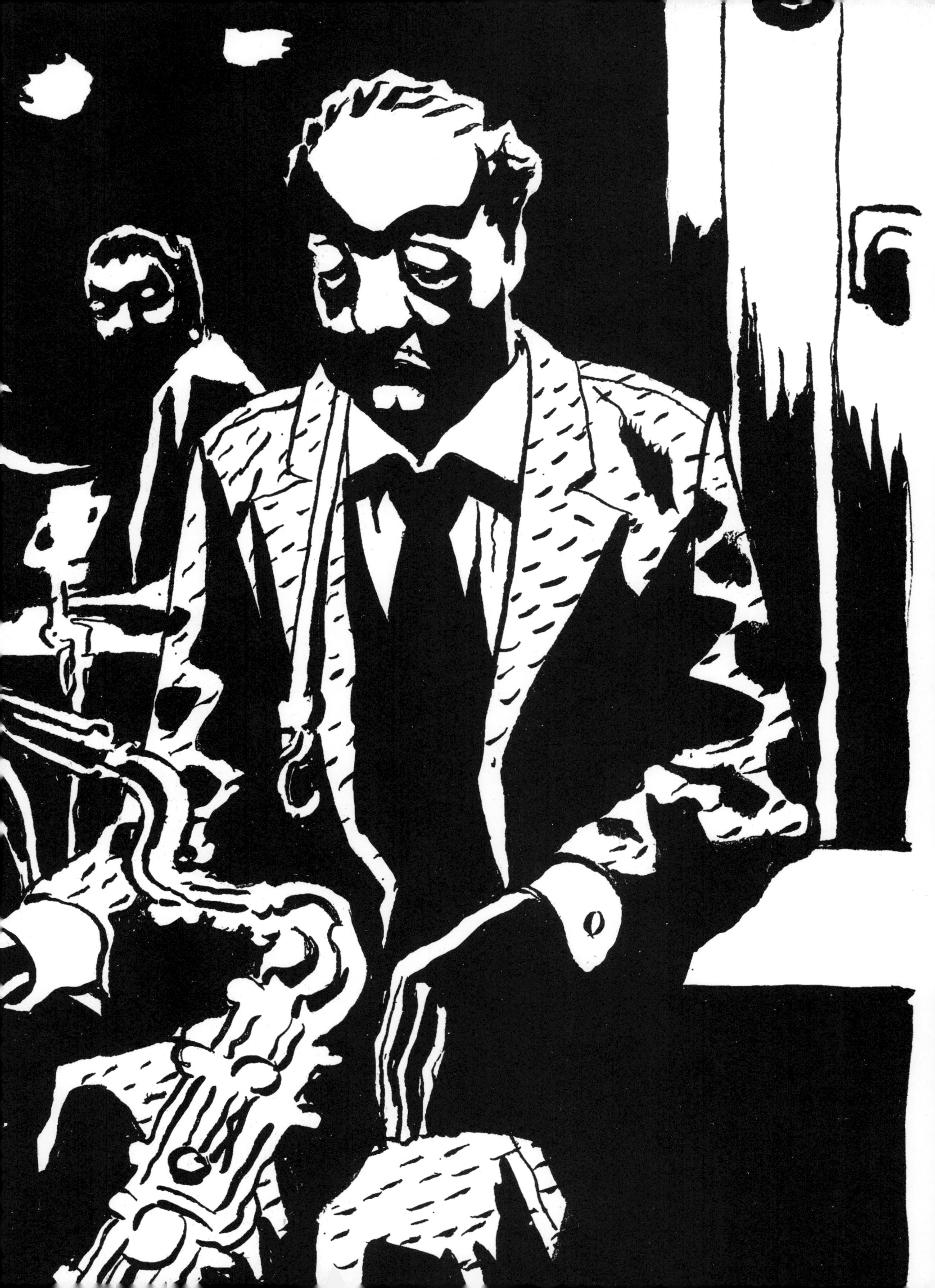

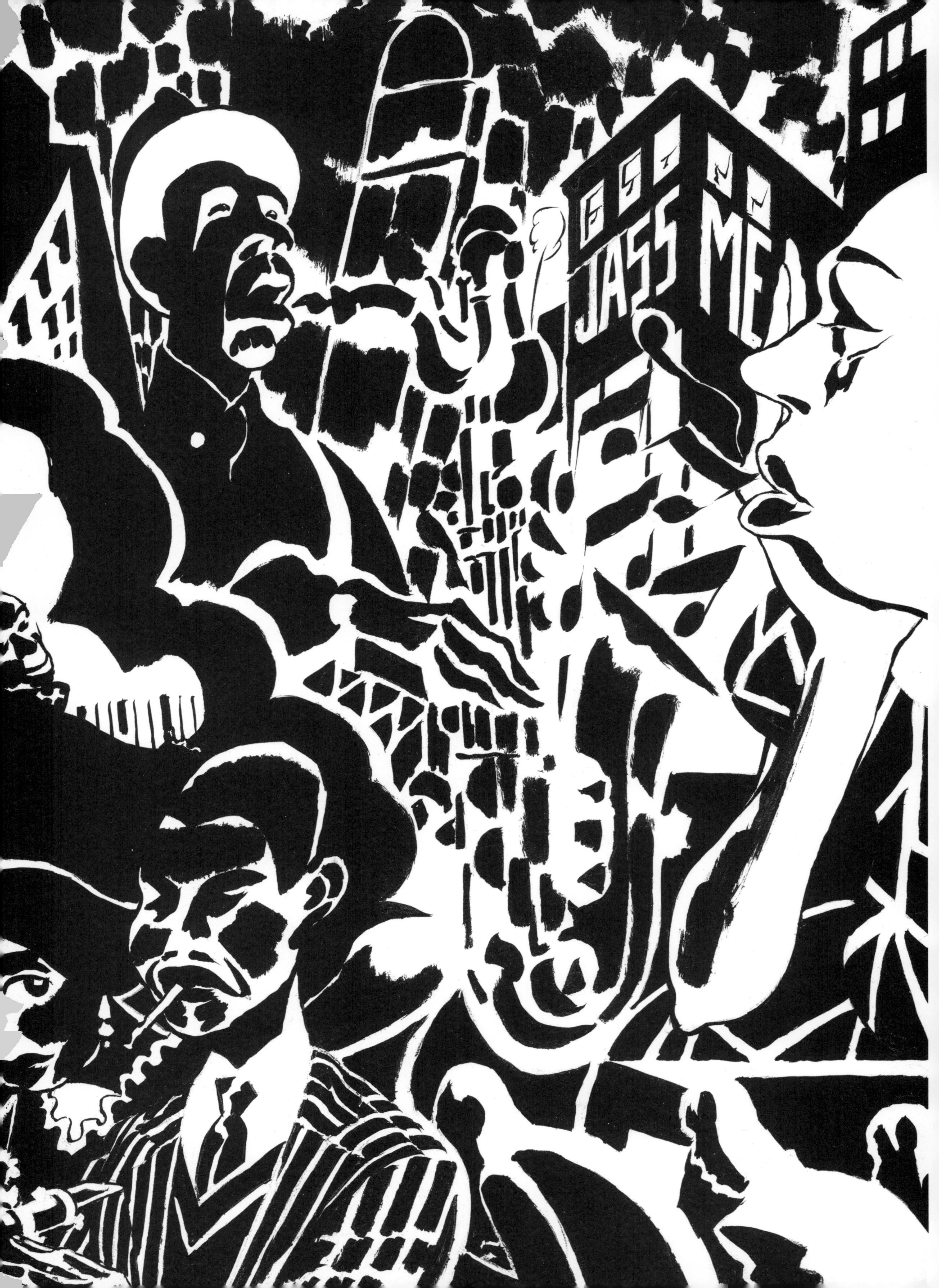
JASS ME

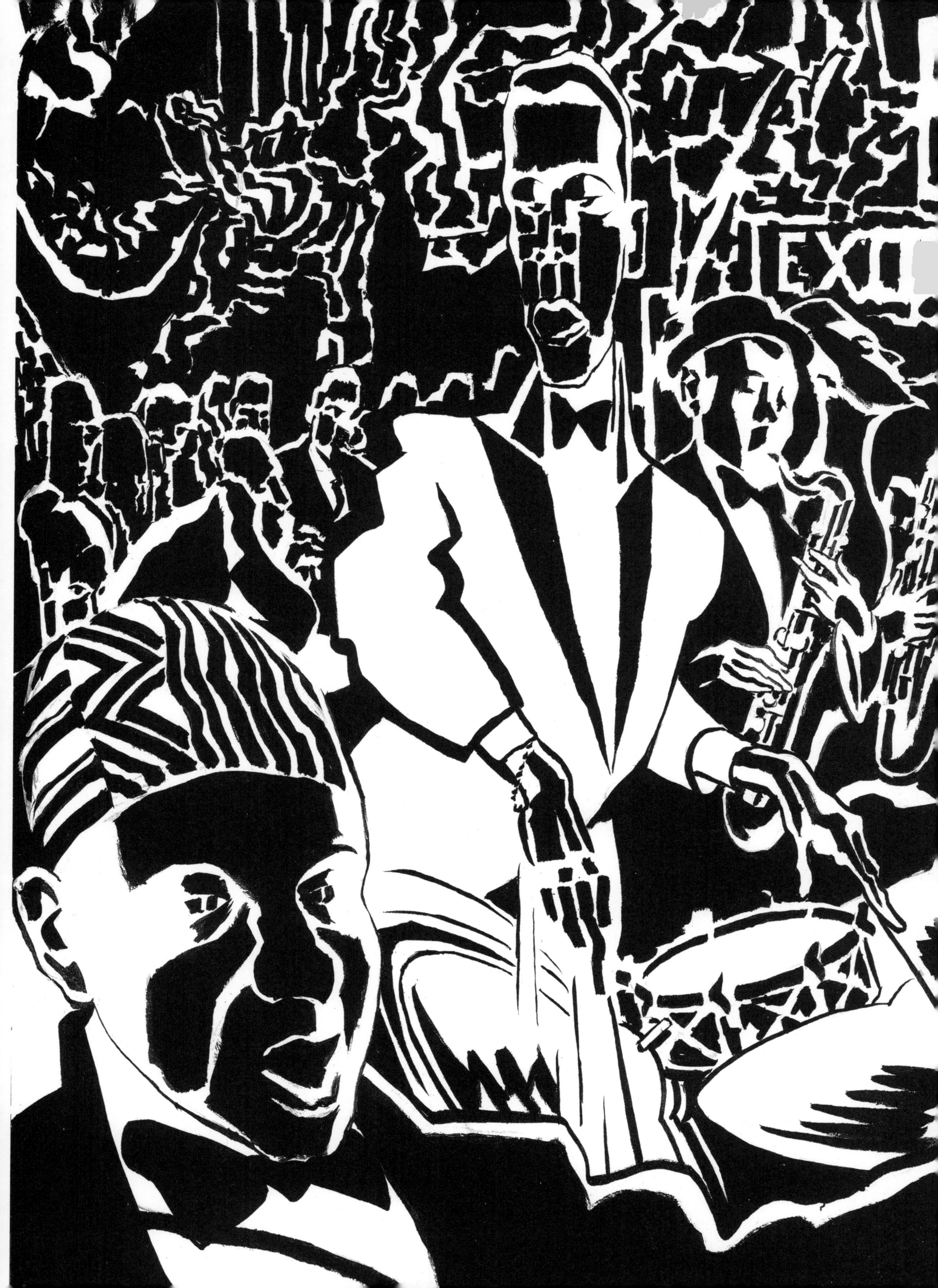

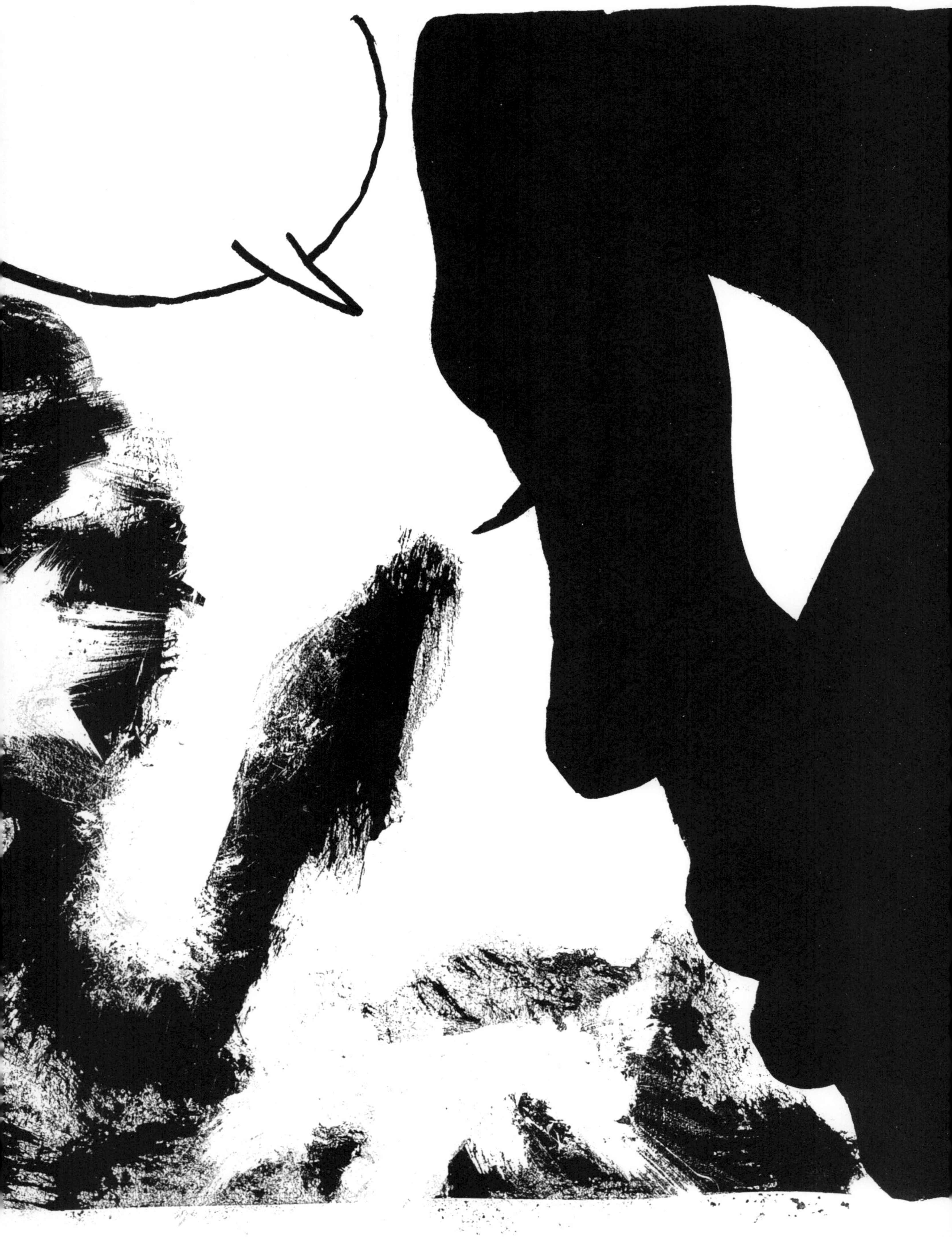